THIS PRESBYTERIAN CHURCH OF OURS

John Congram

Wood Lake Books

Editing: Jim Taylor, Michael Schwartzentruber
Design: Michael Schwartzentruber
Cover design: Lois Huey-Heck

Permissions and acknowledgments
We would like to acknowledge the following sources for their permission to reprint or adapt materials:
Assembly Council for
The Vision Statement (A&P, 1989, p. 201–203)
Living Faith, section 4.2.2
John Moir, *Enduring Witness*
Book of Forms, ordination questions for ministers and elders, section 409–409.4; 412–412.4.

The Presbyterian Church in Canada
Heritage resources
- the diagram on church government
- parts of Jean Stewart's story of the minister catechizing in the home
- Brian Fraser's imaginary interview with Ephraim Scott

Sports Hall of Fame
Photo of James Naismith

Canadian Cataloguing in Publication Data
Congram, John, 1937–
This Presbyterian Church of Ours

ISBN 0–929032–89–6

1. Presbyterian Church—Canada. 2. Presbyterian Church—Doctrines. I. Title.
BX9001.C66 1995 285'.271 C95–910385–6

Published by
Wood Lake Books Inc.
10162 Newene Rd., Winfield, BC
Canada V4V 1R2

Printed in Canada by
Hignell Printing Ltd.
Winnipeg, MB, R3G 2B4

Contents

Preface

For years, whenever I began to read a new book, I carefully read the preface. Usually the authors confessed that they could not have undertaken the monumental task of writing without the love and understanding of their spouse, ten children, three aunts, and two Irish Setters. All of these, they claimed, provided constant support and encouragement. I read and wondered.

I now find myself in an author's position, and I have a deeper appreciation for what they write in their prefaces. Frequently, an author will dedicate a book to a loving, faithful spouse. A few months later I discover they have divorced. Now I understand why.

When I was first asked to undertake this task, I requested time. I used that time to write to friends and colleagues, to ask for their wisdom as to what such a book should contain. Most of them, to my surprise and delight, responded with valuable suggestions. Among those friends and colleagues were Mel Bailey, Ken Barker, Bob Bernhardt, Georgina Caldwell, David Crawford, Zander Dunn, Brian Fraser, Dorcas Gordon, Phil Lee, Sheldon MacKenzie, Joe

McLelland, John Moir, Tony Plomp, and John Vissers.

Sifting through their responses, I found extensive agreement about what the book should contain. All encouraged me to procede.

When the manuscript was nearly completed, I asked a number of laypersons in our church to read it and offer comment and criti-cism. All generously agreed to do this resulting in scores of changes and, I believe, improvements to the manu-script. These people in-cluded Philippa Campsie, Dick Ford, Anne Pennock, Bob Phillips, Dorothy Henderson, Peggy Kipfer, Hugh Lloyd, Lorraine Swaile, Grace and Wally Whyte, and Ivor Williams. Rodger Talbot, who for many years served our church as both missionary and missionary educator, provided invaluable insights into the modern missionary movement.

I have appreciated the opportunity to work under editor Jim Taylor and the good folks at Wood Lake Books, whose idea it was that this book be written. As an editor myself, the experience provided me a much-needed opportunity to walk in another's shoes and to consider the trials and pain of all those writers and contributors to the *Presbyterian Record* who suffer under my editorship.

But more, writing this book made me consider the role of The Presbyterian Church in Canada today. It has given me a new appreciation for what we have been and what we might still be.

And yes, thanks go to my wife, Liz, whom I coerced into reading some of the chapters and who put up with our den in disarray, piled high with books and papers, for over a year. To the great white dog Tasha for giving up some of our quality time together. Appreciation as well to the *Record* committee who allowed me to devote study leave to this project. A final special word of thanks to both professional baseball and hockey for going on strike during much of the writing of this book. Without your help I might never have completed it.

And, yes, any errors or omissions are my responsibility.

I dedicate this book to all the faithful folk of the Presbyterian Church, past and present. Most of their names are not mentioned, perhaps not remembered, but their presence is felt and hereby gratefully acknowledged.

John Congram

Chapter 1

Operating at the margins of modern society
St. Andrew's Presbyterian (LR), Toronto, Ontario.

It's not easy being green—nor Presbyterian

> I stand firmly by the Reformed faith, subject to scripture which I believe cradles God's living Word for those who have ears to hear. That about sums me up—whatever lies before.
>
> —letter from Walter Bryden to Allan Farris
> (Presbyterian Archives)

A 19th-century American once had to explain why he had been tarred and feathered in a small town. The poor fellow told the interviewers that the community had put him to the test on the Monroe Doctrine. "I told them," he said, "that I loved the Monroe Doctrine. I lived by the Monroe Doctrine. I said that I would die for the Monroe Doctrine. I just told them I didn't know what the Monroe Doctrine was."

If reading this book does nothing else for you it should prevent you from ever being tarred and feathered for not knowing what a

Presbyterian is.

Some of you will have started out in some other denomination and may not know much about the Presbyterian Church. Today people pass easily from one denomination to another. Hans Kouwenburg reports that, in January 1990, he conducted a survey of the religious origins of his congregation, St. Giles Presbyterian Church in Prince George, British Columbia. Of the 230 members and adherents, he discovered 58 from a United Church background, 51 Presbyterian or Reformed, 29 Anglican, 19 Lutheran, 19 Baptist, 14 Roman Catholic, 6 Brethren, 6 Pentecostal, 4 Mennonite, and 24 from a variety of other denominations.

In a congregation where I was the minister, we regularly conducted "newcomers' meetings." Held in someone's home, these meetings provided an opportunity for new people in the congregation to get to know each other as well as some of the established members. A fascinating part of each evening occurred when people shared some of their own spiritual journey. We discovered that their passage into Presbyterianism had been triggered by any number of reasons. Some began to attend because they liked the minister, or because their friends or someone who had helped them attended. Or when they moved into the community they wanted to go to a local church and the nearest one turned out to be Presbyterian. Or they came because they wanted their children to be baptized and to grow up in a church school. And, sometimes, a few came because they had specifically sought out a Presbyterian church.

I confess I am one of those who has not always been Presbyterian. In some ways I think this helps me bring a fresh perspective to the subject; it helps me to see both the strengths and weaknesses of the Presbyterian Church. Like some of you, I started out in another denomination.

My introduction to Presbyterianism

I was introduced to Presbyterianism when I was ten. Two decades earlier, my father had left the farm and moved to Toronto. My parents decided to leave Toronto and return to the small southwestern Ontario town of Wingham where they had both grown up. Both of my parents' families had originally come from England and both had deep roots in the Baptist tradition. In fact, the first

Congram who had arrived in 1850 had built the Baptist church in the nearby village of Ripley. However, when my parents arrived back in their hometown, the fires of controversy were raging in the local Baptist church. As a result, they decided we should attend the Presbyterian church. Our participation was always intended as a temporary exile from the Baptist church (our natural home) until the dispute had subsided.

St. Andrew's Presbyterian Church (about half the Presbyterian Churches in Canada bear the name of Scotland's patron saint) became an important part of my life and I never left. Neither did my parents, although I was well on my way to becoming a minister before my parents actually relented, decided they were probably never going to return to the Baptist church, and so became members themselves.

The church building I attended, a tall white brick structure, stood on a small rise set back from the main street in the center of town. Its physical location symbolized both the role it held in the town and its place in my life.

Inside the traditional rectangular sanctuary stood the high central pulpit, a standard feature of most Presbyterian churches of that era. A gallery surrounded three sides of the sanctuary. On the fourth side, the pipes of the organ rose above the pulpit, and the choir and the organist who sat right in front of them, to the ceiling high above.

The pews sat row on straight row in a traditional arrangement, with a center aisle to delight brides. For young children, the most endearing feature of the pews was their elaborate wrought iron ends that allowed the restless or bored to trace endless patterns with their fingers.

Beautiful paintings of angels and archangels with gold scrolls (unusual for Presbyterian simplicity both then as now) covered the walls. No one seemed sure where they had come from, but when a general painting of the building became necessary they were always carefully preserved. After I left to go to university, when the old church was demolished and replaced, I think what I missed most were those paintings.

We usually arrived on the steps of the church as the clock on the post office next door began to chime. The time for worship in those days was unalterably fixed at the sacred hour of 11 o'clock. As the clock chimed our pace quickened and we flew up the stairs to our usual seat in the front of the gallery. Our arrival usually coincided with the entrance of the choir and the singing of the traditional hymn with which every service began: *Holy, Holy, Holy*. This hymn, combined with the same words inscribed in huge letters above the organ pipes on the front wall, left worshipers with no doubt about whom Presbyterians worshiped, or on whom their thoughts should be centered.

If perchance you missed the message, the call to worship God, usually a few sentences from the Bible followed by a psalm—never a hymn—centered our thoughts on some attribute of God: perhaps his power (and it **was** "his" in those days), or majesty, or all-knowingness.

The minister of my growing-up years was a larger-than-life Irishman, Alex Nimmo. Many recruits to the Canadian Church had come from the Presbyterian churches in Ireland and Scotland after the Second World War when there was a shortage of clergy in The Presbyterian Church in Canada. Nimmo was one of them. His sermons never deviated from their 20-minute limit, an attractive and, for those times, unique feature of Presbyterian preaching. Fervor filled each sermon. Although I frequently failed to understand them, I seldom felt bored. I was motivated, if not always enlightened.

Nimmo was the fourth minister of St. Andrew's, the third in 75 years. His immediate predecessor had died while serving St. Andrew's, as would Nimmo himself. The previous minister to these two had stayed for 40 years before retiring. Presbyterians believe in their ministers staying a long time.

Nimmo played a large part in the life of the people of the town in an age before social services. A great portion of his ministry was conducted on the main street. When my friends or I were absent from worship on Sunday, sometime during the following week we could count on being hijacked by his booming voice calling from across main street, "Where were you last Sunday?" His life and example of service influenced me to become a minister.

Such was my introduction to Presbyterianism.

Being green, being Presbyterian

The 1950s and '60s were years of growth and plenty for the church. Chairs often stood beside the pews and filled the aisles to accommodate the crowds who came to worship on Sunday. Even the evening service, by today's standards, would have been considered well-attended. And on baptismal Sunday, the row of babies with their parents stretched from one side of the church to the other. Values considered dear to Presbyterianism were also generally valued in society at large. Most people saw church and society as integral and supportive of each other. I might have been ridiculed in school by the other boys for doing homework, but never for attending church or Sunday school—most of them attended as well.

When I peered over the gallery railing of St. Andrew's, I looked down on the bald pate of John Hanna, member of the (Ontario) provincial parliament; "Doc" Cruickshank, founder and owner of CKNX radio and television; and Eldon McKinney, the mayor of the town. Women, though less prominent in those days, were equally inspirational. Presbyterians were the pillars of the community. Now much of that has changed, not only for Presbyterians, but for all Christians.

Today it is not as easy to be either a Christian or a Presbyterian. Both may find themselves out of sync with society's most highly-prized values. Presbyterians should have empathy with that famous and popular theologian of *Sesame Street,* Kermit the Frog. You will recall the first lines of his hit song, *Bein' Green.*

It's not easy bein' green,
Having to spend the day the color of leaves
I think it could be nicer to be red, yellow, or gold...
It's not easy bein' green like so many ordinary things,
And people tend to pass you over not standing out
Like flashing sparkles in the water or stars in the sky...

As Kermit found it difficult being green, so much in Presbyterianism runs against the grain of modern society. It's not easy being green, and sometimes it's not easy being Presbyterian either. Let me explain.

In an age of instant food, instant solutions, and instant relationships, Presbyterians move slowly and deliberately. Much too slowly for many. You may have heard the old story about the Presbyterian and the light bulb.

Question: How many Presbyterians does it take to change a light bulb?

Answer: Seven. One to change it, six to say they like the old one better.

In a time when the word "law" conjures up all kinds of negative connotations, Presbyterians praise law as a gift from God given for the benefit of God's creatures. We may sometimes dislike the law or rebel against it, but that does not diminish its intrinsic worth as a guide to the good ordering and discipline of our life on earth.

In an age when, if you don't like your church, you can start your own, Presbyterians are unabashedly ecumenical, admitting people to membership in the Holy Catholic Church, recognizing the baptism of other denominations, and practicing open communion (inviting Christians of any denomination to participate in the Lord's Supper).

Swimming against the stream

Presbyterians, in the kind of society in which we live, may be called to be countercultural, to live contrary to or against the prevailing norms and customs of society. In a sense, to be a Christian always calls one to "swim against the stream," to quote the German theologian Emil Brunner. But in particular ways this may be the calling of Presbyterians today. Let me give you a few more examples.

Presbyterians have traditionally been associated with a belief called "the sovereignty of God." This doctrine describes God as being above and "other" than creation. Ultimate power and authority always resides with God. Whatever we may say of God, there is always more. In the Old Testament, Moses was only allowed to see God's back because he could not stand to look upon God's face and live.

Contrast that with the present emphasis on the immanence of God. God is in and a part of all things. God is our buddy and friendly encourager.

A theological professor of mine used to decry what he considered the tendency in the United States to overfamiliarity, not only with God, but with those in authority in the country. It was a period when Americans regularly referred to their president and his wife as Jack and Jackie. My professor dramatized his point by asking us, "What do you think would have happened to the prophet Jeremiah if the people called him Jerry?"

Extreme overfamiliarity with God, represented in some parts of the New Age Movement, can result in human beings viewing themselves as God. That is not to deny that people holding this view point to an important truth. A too-distant concept of God sometimes forgets that Jesus came to earth to make God present and real to God's people.

You shall have no other gods before me

The sovereignty of God also provides a message we lose at our peril. It reminds us that we must never allow a person, institution, or theology to take God's place of ultimate authority. To do so has always led to tyranny and destruction. We should never give an absolute "yes" nor our ultimate allegiance to any human structure, political, philosophical, or social. That place in our lives must be reserved for God alone.

In the early church when Caesar sought to consolidate his empire by having citizens publicly proclaim, "Caesar is Lord," Christians in opposition confessed, "Jesus is Lord." This brief confession, used during baptism, is believed to be the earliest of all Christian creeds. For confessing it, during the early days of the church, many Christians ended up as food for hungry lions.

When Adolf Hitler rose to power in Germany in the 1930s, a young pastor by the name of Dietrich Bonhoeffer felt it necessary to preach a sermon on the first commandment, "You shall have no other gods before me." With great reluctance and after much agonizing, he participated in two abortive attempts to assassinate Hitler. The Gestapo arrested him and sent him to a concentration camp. Just before the end of the war they executed him.

Herbert O'Driscoll believes our present age is a time when affirmations of faith should "be made with all the simplicity and directness of the early church's statement, 'Jesus Christ is Lord.'" Presbyterians, I believe, are called today to witness to that truth.

Presbyterian icebergs

We live in a culture which emphasizes feelings. If it feels right, it **is** right. If it feels okay, do it. Presbyterians, on the other hand, have historically emphasized the mind and reason. An ad in the *Presbyterian Record* pictured a traditional image of Jesus and reminded its readers that "Jesus died to take away our sins not our minds." In an age of feeling, too many Christians act as if Jesus did, in fact, die to take away their minds.

I don't wish to downplay or have Presbyterians ignore the important place of emotions. Presbyterians have sometimes been properly criticized for their lack of genuine warmth and feeling. The 19th century American evangelist D. L. Moody once remarked that, "If you want to see an iceberg you don't have to go to the North Pole, just visit the nearest Presbyterian church."

I remember visiting an elderly gentleman in the hospital. His wife had died the previous year. He told me he had a dream. In it he had died and gone to heaven. There he found himself standing with a crowd on a street corner watching an approaching parade. Bands played, clowns frolicked and handed out balloons to children. Suddenly, he spotted his beloved wife marching in the parade. Before he could rush out and embrace her a hand tapped him on the shoulder. A voice warned, "Sorry, Bob, but we don't do that kind of thing here."

After relating the story, he looked at me and said, "John, if heaven is like that I don't want to go." Who would?

I do not wish to dampen the genuine sharing of joy and sorrow among Christians but rather emphasize what the late Bishop Fulton Sheen noted when he said we had left the rationalistic age and entered the sensate age of feeling. "Never before," he noted, "was truth left so much to the vacillation of an ulcer."

Presbyterians believe their minds and the ability to reason are also God's gifts. Why has God not provided answers to every problem, nor detailed plans for every occasion? Perhaps because God provided us with minds to think and reason, to discover God's will and the path we should follow.

Oriented by and to community

Someone has described our time as an age of "rampant individualism." Others, less kindly, have said it is the age of "me-ism" where everyone puts their own desires and interests first. In the face of that emphasis, Presbyterians remain first and last orientated by and to community. The whole structure on which our church rests, with a series of church courts rather than individuals to direct its life, presumes community.

Sometimes this can become frustrating. Presbyterian church government through a series of courts with equal representation of clergy and laypeople often seems to move at a snail's pace. It often seems quicker and easier to have one person make the decisions rather than a community of people. What Presbyterian at some time has not wished to have a bishop who could make quick decisions in critical situations?

The Presbyterian Moderator, the nearest thing we have to a Pope, is elected only to preside over the highest court, the General Assembly. True, the Moderator remains in office for another year (long enough to install the next Moderator the following year), but the Moderator can only speak for the church in terms of what the community (the church) has already decided. Otherwise, like the editor of the *Presbyterian Record,* Moderators speak only for themselves and, I might add, at their own peril.

Saint Paul's analogy of the church as a body fits the Presbyterian view well. The church is not a whole bunch of individuals each relating to God in isolation from one another. It is a body whose relationship to God is as dependent on the relation of the members of the body to each other, as on their personal devotions.

Wendy Donaldson talks about the time when this insight dawned on her.

> After three years the cancer was back. The doctors said surgery and a high dose of radioactive iodine might stop it. In order to take it I went into isolation. If this was not depressing enough, the known side effect of the drug was depression. This was the low point for me. I was cut off from those whose touch I needed. I was weak and depressed, fearful, and without much hope. But, as a follower of Jesus and a member of a Christian community, I experienced God's care. When I was weak, others were strong and energetic. Meals arrived, child care was arranged. When I lost faith, others believed for me,

offering hope. Into a lonely room full of fear, came a word of reassurance. God was with me. It was a crisis of health, but a revealing of God's purpose for me living in community with other followers of Jesus.

John Calvin, generally considered the founder of Presbyterianism, is seen by some as the instigator of modern capitalism. Calvin had a strong sense of the importance of work. He did not like to waste a minute. Even on his deathbed, when his friends pleaded with him to refrain from his labors, he replied: "What! Would you have the Lord find me idle when he comes?" This work ethic, combined with his sense of the importance of using fully the abilities God gives, provided the congenial environment, some argue, for the rise of capitalism. But what set Calvin apart from much of modern capitalism was his sense of community. The fruits of your labors and abilities should be used to serve and love others, not for your own personal glory, Calvin emphasized.

This emphasis on community also explains why your minister will probably shy away from conducting private baptisms outside the presence of the Christian community. It's not because he or she wishes to be mean, but because the vows parents take at the baptism of their children are not just between themselves and God. The vows also include and are made with the community, in whose presence the young child will grow and without whose presence the vows are unlikely to find fulfillment. In other words, the church community remains integral to our faith and salvation.

Keep your sense of humor and enjoy God

I hope this brief introduction to Presbyterianism will encourage you to explore further what being a Presbyterian means in today's world. It calls for courage. It may mean self-denial and sacrifice. Sometimes you may become frustrated or discouraged. That's okay. It happens to us all. Martin Luther said that in some of his darkest moments all he could do was repeat over and over to himself, "I am baptized." But being part of the Presbyterian family can also bring incredible meaning and purpose to your living.

By the way, there is one other important thing I almost forgot to mention. It's something that Presbyterians have always been in danger of forgetting. In the legitimate effort to take God and their faith seriously, Presbyterians sometimes take themselves too seriously. In the process, they lose the sense of humor and adventure of the life of faith. Popular literature has not helped by perpetuating the caricature of the dour Presbyterian. As a Presbyterian woman said to me recently, "All those kinds of Presbyterians they talk about are gone now." She paused, and then added, "At least I hope they are."

Well, true. But even modern Presbyterians sometimes forget why God has placed them on earth, so eloquently articulated by the answer to the first question of the catechism. Our chief end, it says, is "to glorify God, and to **enjoy** God forever." Presbyterians sometimes come up short on the enjoyment end of things.

In a letter, a friend of mine tells about a conversation he had with a young professional person who no longer goes to church. He was born in a Presbyterian home, was baptized, confirmed, and was a chorister in a Presbyterian congregation while a student in science and medicine. My friend challenged him about his absence from worship or other involvement with the church.

The young person retorted, "Our church places too much emphasis on renunciation for my taste."

Thinking he was using the wrong word, my friend said, "Don't you mean 'denunciation' rather than 'renunciation'?"

"No," he replied, "I'm using the word I want to use in this case. We seem to renounce joy, fun, friendliness, caring, and an intelligent use of scripture and whatever it is we believe about things. But particularly joy and fun."

The conversation, my friend reports, was a sobering one for him and a salient reminder that when we are at our best, we neither renounce nor denounce the great human virtues that keep the rest of the world sane and healthy.

You may recall that at the end of Kermit's song he changes his tune.

But green is the color of spring
Green can be cool and friendly
Green can be big like the ocean
Or important like a mountain
Or tall like a tree...
I'm green and it will do fine

It's beautiful
And I think it's what I want to be.

Sometimes it's not easy being either a Christian or a Presbyterian, especially in the present culture. If you don't like a challenge, maybe you should consider something else. But if, like me, you believe Presbyterianism has an important role to play in the modern world and among other Christian denominations, read on. By whatever route you have come into the Presbyterian family, by the end of the book I hope you will be able to affirm:

"I'm Presbyterian and it will do fine.
It's beautiful.
And I think it's what I want to be."

We will begin our journey by looking at our roots, by exploring where we came from and who our ancestors are.

Chapter 2

Photo: *Presbyterian Record*

Reenactment of the landing of the Hector, Pictou, Nova Scotia.

Roots: the family's history

> A proper pride in and loyalty to one's own tradition are not the opposite of but rather the necessary complement to a wider ecumenical and national loyalty.
>
> —William Klempa
>
> *The Burning Bush and a Few Acres of Snow*, p. 4

A couple of summers ago we vacationed in Nova Scotia. While there, we visited Pictou for the annual reenactment of the landing of the ship, Hector, in 1773. The arrival of the Hector ushered in the first of the great migrations of Highland Scots to the Maritimes. To the Presbyterians in Nova Scotia, who up to that time had no minister of their own, the landing of the Hector was what the landing of the Mayflower was to the Puritans in the 13 colonies. "We venture to say," wrote George Patterson in *A History of Pictou County Nova Scotia*, "that there is no one element in the population

of these Lower Provinces, upon which their social, moral, and religious condition has depended more than upon its Scottish immigrants, and of these that band in the Hector were the pioneers and vanguard."

Each year in Pictou, the Hector arrives complete with locals dressed as the early settlers. Included the year we were there was the local Presbyterian minister together with his family. As you might guess, bagpipes led "the settlers" to the local park where muskets provided a 13-gun salute, followed by speeches by local dignitaries and politicians. An exact replica of the Hector is presently being constructed and will soon take part in this annual gala celebration.

What struck me about the event was the number of people I knew. Presbyterians seemed to appear from under every rock. It was like old home week—and I'm not from Nova Scotia, nor a Scot.

From the arrival of the Hector the continuing immigration of Scots Presbyterians has given Presbyterianism in Canada a decidedly Scottish flavor. The majority of Presbyterian churches in Canada are called St. Andrew's (the patron saint of Scotland) or Knox (the leading figure in the Reformation in Scotland). There are enough Calvins, however, to at least cause you to pause.

The French connection

Sure enough, history records that Presbyterianism began, not with a Scot, but with a French lawyer by the name of John Calvin. Long before the Hector, people who accepted the leadership and teaching of John Calvin arrived on Canadian shores. As a result, the first Presbyterians in Canada were not Scots but Huguenots (the name applied to Reformed French Protestants). Champlain, the famous explorer, married a Huguenot. He and Sieur du Monts, a Huguenot businessman, together founded settlements at St. Croix and Port Royal in 1604.

Both Roman Catholics and Protestants were among the settlers. However, when the Jesuits arrived in 1625 they opposed such toleration granted to the Huguenots as being detrimental to their missionary efforts. As a result, a charter was granted to The Company of the One Hundred Associates organized under Cardinal Richelieu. Part of this charter stipulated that "None but

Frenchmen and Roman Catholics be permitted to settle in the country." This effectively brought to an end settlement in Canada by French Presbyterians.

It is interesting to speculate how Presbyterianism might have been altered if French Presbyterian settlement had been allowed to continue to grow. That the first Presbyterians in Canada were French is worth noting in our present bilingual and multicultural country.

The Frenchman John Calvin also had a direct influence on the course of the Reformation in Scotland through his friend John Knox. Knox was born in a small village a few kilometers from Edinburgh. He attended St. Andrew's University and was ordained a priest in the Roman Catholic Church. When Knox was 15 years old, Patrick Hamilton, a young scholar much taken with the ideas of Luther, was burned at the stake. This memory remained etched in Knox's mind. His favorite Bible passage became John 17 in which Jesus prays for those God has given him, that they will be sustained through the persecutions they would soon face.

Themes of faith and grace introduced to him through the writings of Augustine also swayed Knox's thinking.

On Easter, 1547, Knox preached at St. Andrew's castle. He took the garrison to task for their sins and was surprised when after this they called him to be their pastor.

But two months later the French attacked and captured the castle. They took all of the men, including Knox, to serve as galley slaves.

Nineteen months later Knox was freed and went to England to pastor a congregation. From there he went to Geneva. There he met Calvin and discovered what he described as "the most perfect school of Christ that ever was on earth since the days of the Apostles." It is not surprising, therefore, that, after Knox had spent two years in Geneva, leaders in Scotland invited him to return and to organize the Reformation there. The main tenets and beliefs of the faith Knox transmitted had their origins in the fertile mind and writings of the Frenchman, John Calvin.

Under Knox, Presbyterianism became the major denomination in Scotland.

Presbyterians in Canada

Nearly two centuries later Canada received its first taste of Scottish Presbyterianism when the British captured Louisbourg in 1758. The first Presbyterian worship service conducted in English was led by a Church of Scotland chaplain, Robert McPherson.

When Quebec fell to the British in 1759, Scottish Highland units made up part of Wolfe's army. Again their chaplain, Robert McPherson, conducted Presbyterian worship services for the men. He remained to minister to some of the men who decided to take up permanent residence, although no formal congregation was established at that time.

The first Presbyterian congregation was founded in Quebec City in 1765. At first this congregation worshiped in a room in a Jesuit College. In 1810 the present St. Andrew's building was built. Today, visitors to Quebec often stop off at St. Andrew's, one of the interesting historic sites of the city, which still houses an active, worshiping Presbyterian congregation.

At about the same time, a number of Germans of Calvinist persuasion who were living around Lunenburg tried unsuccessfully to secure a minister from either the old world or the United States. Finally, in June 1770, they took matters into their own hands by ordaining one of their own number, a fisherman by the name of Bruin Romkes Comingoe. Two Presbyterian ministers joined with two Congregational ministers in constituting themselves as the first, if somewhat irregular, presbytery to ordain Comingoe. The ordination was carried out in the Dissenters' Chapel in Halifax, which became the nucleus for what, in turn, became St. Matthew's Church. This action was significant not only because it was the first action by a presbytery in Canada, but because it reflected the ecumenical spirit at the heart of Presbyterianism and the potential in Presbyterianism to be flexible to meet new challenges.

An event which would shape much of early Presbyterianism occurred in 1786 when the Church of Scotland appointed James MacGregor as a missionary to Pictou, Nova Scotia. But the action shocked MacGregor. "It put me into such confusion," he wrote, "that I did not know what to say or think. I had considered it a clear case, not to myself only, but to the majority of the synod, that I was called to preach to the Highlanders of Scotland..."

Even after he had arrived in Pictou on July 22, 1786, he was not sure this was where he should be. He later described his feelings: "I looked on myself as an exile from the church and society... Nothing but necessity kept me there; for I durst not think of encountering the dangerous road to Halifax again, and there was no vessel in Pictou to take me away."

Despite this rough beginning, MacGregor proceeded to minister in the Maritimes for 44 years. He traveled throughout Prince Edward Island, Cape Breton, and New Brunswick, ministering to all he met. He urged the Scottish church to send out more ministers.

He asked his own congregation to provide practical support for new immigrants. He, himself, provided each new immigrant with a shovel and axe if they needed them.

One of his most famous acts was an open letter he wrote to the Rev. Mr. Cock of Truro, Nova Scotia, who owned a slave girl. MacGregor eloquently made the case against slavery but did more than that. He spent £20 from his first year's salary of £27 to buy the slave girl's freedom.

MacGregor, perhaps more than any other person, helped to establish the Presbyterian church in Nova Scotia and to open the way for a steady stream of ministers to the colony over the next decades.

Up until 1843, as settlers flooded into Canada, Presbyterianism grew largely as a result of immigration from Ireland and Scotland. At this time there still was no indigenous or independent Presbyterian Church in Canada. The church in Canada was a branch plant of the Church of Scotland.

In 1843, the Church of Scotland divided over the relationship the church ought to have with the state. A new Presbyterian church, the Free Church was born. Unlike Scotland, where the Church of Scotland was the official church in the country, Canada had no official or state church. Despite this, Presbyterian churches in Canada, because they were largely made up of Scottish settlers, were profoundly affected by this decision taken in Scotland. Although it had no practical relevance in Canada, many believed an important theological principle was at stake. As a result, Presbyterian bodies in Canada tended to separate on the same basis as those in Scotland.

Despite these quarrels which spilled over into Canada from Scotland, the next 30 years were productive years for Presbyterian growth in Canada. The division in Scotland resulted in increased missionary activity in Canada as now **two** Presbyterian churches, the Church of Scotland and the Free Church, sent ministers and established congregations and colleges in Canada.

Have you ever noticed that in the same town or city you will sometimes discover two Presbyterian churches on opposite corners or across the street from each other? Quite often you will find one called Knox and the other St. Andrew's. These two congregations were probably originally established by the two rival branches of Presbyterianism in Scotland. The Church of Scotland tended to call congregations they established, St. Andrew's, while the Free Church preferred to name theirs after the reformer, John Knox.

The year 1848 marks an important event in Canadian Presbyterian history. In that year the first missionary was sent from Canada by Presbyterians. With the support of all the synods of the Maritimes, John Geddie began his work among the aboriginals of the New Hebrides islands. After he died, his congregation in the New Hebrides erected a memorial tablet with the inscription, "When he landed, in 1848, there were no Christians here, and when he left, in 1872, there were no heathen."

In 1851, John Black was sent as a missionary to the Selkirk settlers on the banks of the Red River in Manitoba. They had been waiting for a minister since 1811. This settlement, under the long ministry of John Black until his death in 1882, became the base for the evangelization of the West.

From here James Nisbet, after serving as Black's assistant, went out to serve the Crees on the North Saskatchewan River. He founded the city of Prince Albert and attempted to educate the Crees to the white man's ways through vocational training, believing this to be the only avenue for their survival.

The Presbyterian Church in Canada...

During this period, in response to the need for a more effective and unified missionary effort, a series of unions took place among the various factions of Presbyterians in Canada. It became increasingly clear that the divisions that separated the church in Scotland were irrelevant in Canada. These divisions were mainly over the relationship of the state to the church. The Church of Scotland was prepared to accept both advice and financial support from the state. Some of the Free churches would accept money but not advice, while others would accept neither advice nor money. But in Canada, with no state church, this issue was immaterial.

By 1875 a series of unions had left only four separate Presbyterian bodies in Canada. Two were divided by geography, and two were still divided by the old church-state controversy. On June 25, 1875, in Montreal, these final four Presbyterian groups united to form The Presbyterian Church in Canada. The new union included 88,000 members, 600 ministers, and 700 congregations.

Even then, the name, The Presbyterian Church in Canada, was not totally descriptive of this new church. A few years earlier, St. Andrew's Church in Hamilton, Bermuda, decided to link up with the Presbytery of Halifax. St. Andrew's had been started by Christ Church (Church of Scotland) but decided, for matters of convenience and conflict, to associate with the Canadian church. Today, St. Andrew's forms a part of the Presbytery of West Toronto, airline links between Canada and Bermuda making this the most feasible connection.

Don Corbett, former principal of Knox College, used to joke that if Quebec ever left Canada we would have to change our name from The Presbyterian Church **in** Canada, to The Presbyterian Church **in and out of** Canada. In fact, from the beginning, the latter term has been more descriptive of our church. Not surprising, that Bermudians often feel ignored and forgotten by the national church.

Between 1875 and 1925 Presbyterianism in Canada experienced unprecedented growth. Synods (usually a large geographical area comprising several presbyteries) increased from four to eight, presbyteries from 33 to 79, ministers from 602 to 1708, and communicant membership from 88,000 to 380,000.

Growth was particularly evident in the West under the aggressive leadership of James Robertson who had been appointed Home Mission Superintendent. Some were suspicious of the office of superintendent which they felt smacked of episcopal (hierarchical) order, especially under Robertson's constant demands for more money and resources. An alleged remark to his wife regarding ministerial recruits for the West typified his approach to the work. He would, he apparently said, "rather have a man know less Latin and more horse." Robertson, more than any other person, was responsible for making the Presbyterian church the largest denomination in the West before most Presbyterians joined with the Methodists and Congregationalists to form the United Church of Canada in 1925.

...and abroad

John Moir, in his book on Presbyterian history entitled *Enduring Witness*, describes the last half of the 19th century and the first part of the 20th century as "the great age of missions." Not only was there great growth and consolidation of the faith in Canada, but a host of new mission fields were opened overseas beginning with the appointment of John Geddie in 1846 to the New Hebrides and the many who followed him there.

Moir talks about the establishment of the various missions and notes the extent of their growth by 1914, as follows.

- After a visit to Trinidad, Rev. John Morton persuaded the Synod of the Lower Provinces to send him back as a missionary in 1867. By 1914 the mission had grown to include 66 day schools, two theological colleges, two ordained East Indians, and 50 catechists (laypersons with some training in ministry).
- Interest in Trinidad led to the establishment of a mission in British Guiana in 1885. By 1914 British Guiana (now Guyana) had 22 mission stations, five missionaries, and 21 East Indian workers.
- In 1872, George Leslie Mackay went to Formosa and three years later there were nine chapels, 400 worshipers, three schools, and nine native helpers. By 1914, 21 Canadians served there with 77 native helpers.
- In 1888, the students of Knox College sent Jonathan Goforth to mainland China, and Queens sent J. Fraser Smith. By 1914, 74 Canadian Presbyterians were serving in China. Additional areas of work were opened in Shanghai with the Christian Literature Society, and in Shantung province. An additional 88 Canadians served in these areas.

Missionary activity begun in India and Korea during this period met with similar success.

One day in the 1950s, a delegation from Japan arrived in my home town of Wingham, Ontario. They said they had come to visit the grave of Caroline Macdonald. The locals looked in puzzlement at each other. They did not know whom the delegation was talking about. Most had completely forgotten one of Wingham's most famous daughters.

Caroline Macdonald was born and went to school in Wingham. After graduating from the University of Toronto in 1901, she became general secretary of the Young Women's Christian Association (YWCA) of Ottawa. After the YWCA decided to open Christian work in the Far East, Caroline Macdonald was appointed as National Secretary for Japan. She established several hostels for women during the first few years in Japan.

An unexpected tragedy in Tokyo changed her life. A young man who attended her Bible class committed a murder in a fit of jealousy. She began to visit him in prison. So impressed was the governor of the prison that he requested her to visit 30 prisoners on death row. From this began Caroline Macdonald's work in the prisons throughout Japan visiting, comforting, and sharing God's love with the inmates. The Japanese gave her the nickname "The White Angel of Tokyo." Her sacrificial work in the prisons of Japan resulted, many years later, in the delegation arriving in Wingham to pay homage at her grave.

In many ways, Caroline Macdonald symbolized all of the best in the missionary enterprise during this period.

Church Union

But the very success of the missionary enterprise led some during this period to begin to question whether denominations themselves were relevant any longer. Could not more be accomplished with all the denominations working as one? When Church Union came to Canada in 1925 Presbyterian missionaries overwhelmingly supported it. To Canadian Presbyterians, the old divisions in Scotland seemed increasingly irrelevant, and John Black had noted the confusion caused to the native mind by having so many brands of Christianity.

Presbyterians took the first concrete step toward the union of all the churches when, in 1899, at the request of the national board responsible for missions, a committee was appointed "to confer with representatives of other evangelical churches, having power to enter into an arrangement with them that will tend to bring about a more satisfactory state of things in our Home Mission Fields so that overlapping, complained of, may be prevented."

As a result of this action, consultations and meetings were held mainly with the Methodists and Congregationalists. Some strongly favored an organic union which would produce a national church. Others argued for a kind of federation under which denominations would cooperate but retain their own identity. Supporters of this view felt it could prevent a serious disruption in the Presbyterian church. Successive votes on the question of union increasingly indicated that a serious disruption was a real possibility.

In the end, the forces favoring organic union won the day. On the final day of General Assembly on June 9, 1925, the following resolution was adopted:

> that when this Assembly adjourns this afternoon it do adjourn to meet in College Street Presbyterian Church at the hour of nine o'clock in the morning, on Wednesday, the twenty-fourth day of June, 1925, unless in the meantime its rights, privileges, authorities, and powers shall have ceased under the terms of section 22(a) of the United Church of Canada Act...

When this act of the federal government came into effect at midnight that evening, 79 dissenting commissioners had already chosen a new Moderator and were meeting in General Assembly in Knox Church, Toronto.

The next day 8,000 people watched in the Mutual Street Arena as the United Church of Canada was inaugurated with the signing of the Basis of Union. Rev. George Pidgeon, who became the first Moderator of the United Church, signed for the Presbyterians. The new church brought together nearly 100 percent of the Congregationalists and Methodists in Canada, together with more than 60 percent of the Presbyterians. Before Union, Congregationalists claimed 12,586 members, Methodists 384,845, and Presbyterians 379,762. In 1926, the United Church reported 609,729 members, the Presbyterians 163,374.

In a later chapter we will discuss some of the pros and cons of this union and why so many Presbyterians stayed out. Suffice it to say here that in the wake of the union both churches faced a difficult period of adjustment and bitterness. The Presbyterian Church had more congregations than ministers; the United Church more ministers than it could employ. Because each congregation could vote on whether or not it wished to enter union, minority groups on both sides often found themselves without a church building. Ironically, sometimes the Presbyterian congregation would purchase the now vacant Methodist church, while the new United Church occupied the former Presbyterian building. Property went to the majority even if that majority was only 51 percent.

In the small village of Bluevale, Ontario, the Unionists won the vote. The new United Church began meeting in the former Presbyterian building. Only one thing had not been passed on to the new United Church—the actual architectural plans for the Presbyterian church building. The following year, when the continuing Presbyterians rebuilt, they used the same plans to build their new church that had been used to build the previous one. Today in Bluevale, two almost identical buildings stand around the corner from each other, the only difference being that the Presbyterian one is slightly newer.

Ruth Tingle was 20 years old when Church Union came to her hometown of Ingersoll, Ontario. She remembers the terrible stress and strain it caused in families and the community, and the deep lingering suspicion which continued for years afterwards. Her father, at the time the superintendent of the Sunday school in the Presbyterian church, told his family that if Church Union were successful they would join the Anglican Church.

Hugh Lloyd was a young boy at the time of Union. His father was the Presbyterian minister in Midland, Ontario. He remembers sitting in the parlor when guest ministers came to call, and listening to them rail against the injustices perpetrated against Presbyterians in the wake of Church Union.

Difficulties were experienced on the international scene as well. Delegations from both the United Church and the Presbyterian Church arrived at the meetings of the World Alliance of Reformed Churches, both claiming to represent The Presbyterian Church in Canada.

Happily, since 1925, the relations between the two denominations have steadily improved until today you often find congregations at the local level sharing summer services as well as participating together in social and justice issues.

In 1994, when the United Church sold the building which had been their headquarters and prepared to move to rental accommodation, they invited other denominations to consider moving in with them. The fact that Presbyterians seriously considered making this move shows how attitudes between the two churches have improved.

It is also important to note at this point that although many Presbyterians did not enter the Union the decision did not mean they were antiecumenical or unwilling to cooperate with other denominations in mission and outreach. To make this point, the General Assembly of 1947 passed a resolution, sponsored by militant antiunionist F. Scott MacKenzie, affirming Presbyterians' belief in the one holy, catholic, and apostolic church, repudiating sectarianism, and declaring its willingness to engage in joint ventures with other denominations for the sake of Christ's kingdom.

The division of institutions and mission fields had to be negotiated between the two churches. Of the seven Presbyterian theological colleges, only Knox College in Toronto and Presbyterian College in Montreal remained within the Presbyterian Church. The irony of this is that Knox College had been specifically constructed to be the college of the new union church.

Before Union, the Presbyterian church supported missionaries on eight fields: Trinidad, British Guiana, India (two fields), Formosa, North and South China, and Korea. After Union, responsibility continued for missions in British Guiana, parts of India, Formosa, and among the Koreans in Japan. The fields in China were divided between the two denominations.

Immediately after Church Union the Presbyterian Church tended to turn in on itself, faced as it was with the tremendous task of rebuilding a shattered organization. In many places, but particularly in the West, Presbyterian churches no longer existed.

Out of the events of 1925, and in many ways still dominated by them, the Presbyterian Church stumbled into the Great Depression of the 1930s and then into the Second World War. The One Step Forward Movement, whose goal was to raise $180,000, brought in only $62,000 in one and a half years. A Diamond Jubilee Thank Offering, begun in 1935 to raise $206,000, succeeded in raising only $46,000 in two years. The Scott Institute, initiated and operated largely through the efforts of Presbyterian minister Morris Zeidman, a converted Jew, was feeding 1,000 men a day in Toronto during the '30s. But in 1941, alleging unfair and unnecessary interference by the hierarchy of the denomination, Zeidman pulled out of the Presbyterian Church and established the Scott Mission as an independent entity. A campaign initiated by the United Church to send freight cars of food and clothing to desperate people in the West elicited only three carloads from the Presbyterians.

In his book *Enduring Witness*, John Moir reported that by 1945 the Presbyterian Church

> remained very much what it had been a generation earlier—the church of an urban minority, predominantly English-speaking and 'Anglo-Saxon,' heavily concentrated in the eastern and central provinces. In 1926 it had 45 presbyteries—in 1946 it reported only one more. Its membership in 1926 had been 160,000—20 years later that figure had grown by only one percent, a figure that could not be, like finances, blamed on the Depression.

Signs of new life

A number of factors following the Second World War resulted in some remarkable changes in the church. Along with other major denominations, Presbyterians benefited from the upsurge in church attendance during the 1950s and '60s. As new suburban areas sprang up Presbyterians actively established many new congregations.

Another indication of new life in the church occurred in 1957 when the church opened Armagh in Clarkson, Ontario, to provide a home for unwed mothers. In 1992, Armagh was rededicated as a shelter for battered women and their children.

In the '60s, the church faced the question of women in ministry, deciding on June 9, 1966, that women should be ordained both to the ruling and teaching eldership. On May 29, 1968, in Appin, Ontario, Shirley Jeffrey became the first woman ordained to the ministry of Word and Sacraments in The Presbyterian Church in

Canada. Others were quick to follow. Today nearly one half of all candidates studying in our colleges are women.

Thirteen years after the ordination of the first woman, a dispute over the issue arose in the Presbytery of East Toronto. While being interviewed in preparation for his ordination by the presbytery, Dan MacDougall declared he would not participate in the ordination of women. After a long debate the presbytery refused to ordain him.

Those who defended MacDougall argued that on such matters as this there should be "liberty of conscience," that people who could not accept the ordination of women should not have to participate in such ordinations. After appeals to the General Assembly and special commissions appointed to consider the issue, in 1982, the General Assembly ruled that those who were already ministers of the church have freedom of belief on the question of the ordination of women, but do not have freedom of action. The church had spoken decisively and unequivocally on the issue.

The first ruling elder to be ordained was Joan McInnis of St. Andrew's Church in Arthur, Ontario. She was elected only three days after the General Assembly made its decision to allow the ordination of women. Her first response to the idea of becoming an elder was a flat, "No." "My generation," she explained, "was raised to believe women did not do that kind of thing."

But to an observer, it was no surprise when Joan was elected an elder. She played leading roles in many church groups, including the choir, the church school, and a church drama group. She symbolized and embodied the critical role women had always played in the church, a role often unrecognized.

In retrospect, she feels women have special gifts to bring to the eldership and to the situations they must address—gifts such as compassion and tenderness. She believes that women are often easier to approach than men, and frequently they are better listeners.

Also in the 1960s, the pace of missionary activity increased overseas and the way mission was done began to undergo a radical shift. In the Presbyterian Church these years were dominated by the person and prophetic witness of E.H. Johnson. He, more than most of his contemporaries, sensed the direction in which the world was moving and the opportunities it presented to the church. He encouraged the development of indigenous churches and a changed position for the missionary to a supportive role to leaders in the indigenous church. He set in motion a vigorous program of missionary education within the church in Canada, a program which brought the reality of missionary activity to ordinary Presbyterians. Before others, he saw the future role of China in the world and pioneered the reestablishment of relations between the church in China and western churches after a long period without communication.

The Presbyterian Church in Nigeria was the first new partner in Africa after the Second World War. When the Nigerian civil war broke out, Johnson, who was by then in charge of overseas missions, mobilized a massive relief effort to help the Biafrans. (The Biafrans were a group who rebelled against the central government and who were ultimately defeated after much bloodshed and starvation.) Planes were rented, a relief team which included three Presbyterians was sent to Nigeria, and $141,000 was raised for the relief effort by the church in just six months.

Some of the new missionaries to Nigeria, such as Ron McGraw, Earle Roberts, and Russell Hall, played an important and sometimes dangerous role during the Biafran War by bringing relief supplies and assistance to many of its sufferers.

Traditional partnerships in India, Guyana, and Taiwan were renewed and strengthened, and new partners accepted in Nigeria and Japan. By supporting indigenous churches, Canadian Presbyterians played significant roles in the formation of the Church of North India, the Korean Christian Church in Japan, and the Guyana Presbyterian Church.

In Japan, Donald and Marion Powell helped to build links between spread-out Korean congregations, an effort that helped in the formation of the Korean Christian Church in Japan. Missionaries such as Beth and Jack McIntosh fought for years against the Japanese government's hated fingerprinting law. This law required all foreigners (defined under the Japanese Registration Law) to be fingerprinted. This included ethnic Koreans who had lived in Japan for generations. McIntosh stood with his Korean friends in refusing to be fingerprinted. His actions helped that church to grow into one of the strongest smaller churches in East Asia.

In more recent years, new partnerships have been established with the Church of Central Africa in Malawi, and the Presbyterian Church in Mauritius. In 1970, John and Ruth Reoch were the first to go to a new mission field in Afghanistan.

The newest of our partnerships are with the Presbyterian Church in Mozambique, and the part of the Lesotho Evangelical Church which is in South Africa and is known as the Evangelical Church of South Africa. Both of these churches were begun by the French Swiss Reformed Church.

Our involvement in Canadian Church Coalitions led to a deeper involvement in Central America. Under the direction of Joe Reed, many Canadian Presbyterians have become familiar with justice issues in Central America.

Today, nearing the end of the 20th century, the Presbyterian Church remains eager to play its full part in the mission of the church, cooperating fully with other Christian denominations in this great task.

Encouraged by the past, we look to the future

In 1872, George Grant, a one-armed Presbyterian minister from Halifax, accompanied Sandford Fleming across Canada to map out the route for the proposed transcontinental railway. Grant served as the secretary of the expedition, his humorous and colorful account of which was published under the title *Ocean to Ocean*. Near the end of the book he exclaims,

> ...there is one Gospel for and unto all; nothing less than this was the thought—deeply felt if sometimes inarticulately expressed—of our great ancestors in the brave days of Old. And it is ours also.

And then a little later,

> ...We come of a race that never counted the number of its foes, nor the number of its friends, when freedom, loyalty, or God was concerned.

Encouraged by our past, the Presbyterian family expects to continue to make history in the 21st century. Not in any self-confident or self-assured way, but in faith and hope that Christ who continues to lead the way has called us to follow.

Chapter 3

Henry Meylan

John Calvin

Photo: *Presbyterian Record*

Laszlo Tokes

Reformed and reforming: what the Presbyterian family believes

Q: What is the chief end of man?
A: Man's chief end is to glorify God, and to enjoy him forever.

—the first question in *The Shorter Catechism*

"In the Vargas' home, Margit, standing by the window, turned on the radio and heard the news.

'Mummy,' demanded her small daughter, 'why are you crying?'

'Because communism is over,' she replied."

Romania, Christmas Day, 1989
—David Porter, *With God, for the People*

The Reformed faith, when it has been believed and acted upon, has always had the power to produce people of great courage and resourcefulness. Take the case of Laszlo Tokes, the Reformed pastor in Romania who became the spark to light the revolution which overthrew the cruel dictator Nicolae Ceausescu.

Tokes faced not only a hostile world, but also a church leadership which had become the puppet of the regime, as the following story illustrates.

It was not the first time Pastor Laszlo Tokes had been summoned to Bishop Papp's office. (Some European Reformed and Presbyterian churches have bishops. This goes back to times in these countries when only the aristocracy and bishops were given a voice in parliament.) It would not be the last.

> "Pastor Tokes," the bishop began, "you are giving me cause for concern. Cause for considerable concern," he added.
>
> "In what regard?" Tokes inquired.
>
> "You are permitting the membership to grow too quickly. You are drawing too much attention to the church."
>
> "It is hard to prevent them coming, Bishop."
>
> "You could stop them. It is you they come to hear. The city is full of talk about the new preacher at the Reformed church. Your fine speaking voice."
>
> "What is happening is happening by the hand of God, Bishop. Perhaps he makes use of skills he gave me. But it is not because of me that people come."

After a series of threats, often wrapped up in what Tokes described as a "kind of spiritual exhortation," Bishop Papp concluded the interview with these words: "Remember what I have said, Pastor Tokes. I do not speak only for myself. I have contacts with the Ceausescu family, you know."

Tokes comments, "I tried not to stoop as I left."

(Adapted from the book by David Porter, *With God, for the People*, Hodder & Stoughton, 1990.)

Many events have taken place in Romania in the few years since that incident. At Christmas 1989, Bishop Papp found himself barricaded in the manse in Nagyvarad, surrounded by an angry mob prepared to lynch him. A call went out to local clergy to come to protect their bishop. Eventually, he escaped to France where he still resides.

After those events, Laszlo Tokes was elected bishop, succeeding his tormentor. He moved into the house from which Papp had so recently fled. The word "Judas," painted on the walls of the manse, was still visible when Tokes and his family took up residence there in May 1990.

To us it seems inconceivable that a minister could be disciplined, exiled, even removed from the ministry, for teaching the gospel to the young, for conducting Bible studies and for creating a lively, growing congregation. But that was the reality of life in Reformed congregations in Romania before the revolution. Ceausescu and his secret police rigorously controlled all of life, including the church. Church officials, especially people such as bishops, required the approval of the state before they were appointed. Unless they were willing to compromise, there was no chance of them being appointed to positions of influence, or of them remaining in those positions for long. Laszlo Papp was perhaps the worst example of this system in the Reformed Church in Romania. He was a bishop who sought power and personal survival rather than the service of God and the people.

The focus for the people's long pent-up rage and frustration, both with the cruel Ceausescu regime and a church which, for the most part, feared and obeyed it, finally found its expression in one man in Romania who refused to buckle under. Laszlo Tokes stood against the abuse of both church and state, and encouraged his people to do the same.

Tokes was largely unknown to the outside world before the cataclysmic events of December 1989. A year prior to the revolution, a Canadian television crew had interviewed him. Having risked their lives to get the interview, they found no outlet in North America willing to show it. Again and again they were met with rejection: "Who's interested in listening to an obscure Romanian pastor talk about freedom?" Soon afterward, Tokes' name became a household word. The defiance of this obscure pastor against the Ceausescu regime roused a nation to rebel.

Oliver Cromwell is reported to have said that he would rather face an army with fixed bayonets than one Calvinist who was convinced he was doing God's will. This has been both the blessing and curse of Presbyterianism. In the case of Laszlo Tokes, blessing.

I thought of this recently as I watched the installation of Nelson Mandela as the new President of South Africa. F.W. de Klerk, former president now to become the vice president, stood beside him. The wonderful story of Mandela's rise from political prisoner to president boggles the mind. Lesser-known but no less amazing is the story of Frederick de Klerk. Grandson of one of the patriarchs of the Boer War, son of a cabinet minister in the government that fashioned apartheid, he had the courage to begin dismantling apartheid and negotiating himself out of power. In an article in the *New Yorker* (April 8, 1994), writer Allister Sparks speaks of the religious motivation of de Klerk and his sense of call to this task. This too is Calvinism at its finest.

Laszlo Tokes, a pastor in the Reformed Church in Romania, Frederick de Klerk, a member in the Dutch Reformed Church in South Africa—both members of a large family of churches which bear the name Reformed or Presbyterian.

The word "Reformed" forms a part of the official name of some of these churches. For example, the Reformed Church of France. Another group of churches, including The Presbyterian Church in Canada, has "Presbyterian" as a part of their official name. Both groups form a part of the same family held together under an umbrella known as the World Alliance of Presbyterian and Reformed Churches. This alliance held its first meeting in Edinburgh, Scotland, in 1877. Today it includes over 70 million members worldwide in nearly 200 churches in over 90 countries.

"Reformed" refers to what the denomination believes; "Presbyterian" refers to its polity or how it is organized.

Reformed and reforming

Often the phrase used to describe this branch of the church is "reformed and reforming." Actually, the origin of this phrase is lost in obscurity. It is unlikely any of the reformers, including John Calvin, ever used it. Gisbert Foetus, a theologian, used a similar phrase, "the church always reforming because it is reformed," in the early 17th century. Probably when first used it related primarily to the necessity of the reform of human life. Certainly none of the early reformers would have used the phrase to advocate any change not in conformance to the authority of scripture.

Today it is most often used to signify Presbyterians' belief that the Reformation was not complete in the 16th century. In fact, Presbyterians believe the process of reform is never complete. There is no time that represents a golden or perfect age in the church. Not Calvin's time. Not even the first century under the Apostles.

To be a Presbyterian means you believe in an open system—one that moves—a church not exempt from God's judgment. A church which, as Augustine said, must also pray, "Forgive us our sins." Reformed, yes, but also always in the process of being reformed.

John Calvin

As I mentioned earlier, the founder of this Reformed or Presbyterian part of the church was a French lawyer by the name of John Calvin. Calvin was a young boy growing up in Noyon, France, an area about 100 kilometers northeast of Paris, when Martin Luther launched the Protestant Reformation by nailing 95 theses to the church door in Wittenberg in 1517. Although he had his differences with Luther and never met him personally, Calvin always admired Luther. Calvin wrote to his friend Heinrich Bulling and said, "even if he [Luther] were to call me a devil, I should still regard him as an outstanding servant of God."

Calvin's father, a lawyer who worked for the church, intended that his son should enter the priesthood. At the University of Paris where he studied philosophy, Calvin encountered such church luminaries of the time as Loyola and Xavier. At age 19 he began studying law at Orleans and Bourges. In his mid 20s he was imprisoned briefly for expressing Protestant convictions.

Like many of the other reformers, Calvin never wanted to leave the church of Rome. He simply wanted it reformed in line with the principles and life of the church reflected in the pages of the Bible. Before he died Calvin gave strict instructions that he be buried in a common cemetery with no tombstone. He did not want to give any encouragement to those who might want to form a religion around him or make his grave into a shrine. Today the site of his grave remains unknown.

In 1534 Calvin sought refuge from persecution in Basel, Switzerland, where the Reformation was already well-established. While there, when he was 26 years old, he published a study guide on the faith called the *Institutes of the Christian Religion*. Through it he sought to present a reasoned and logical exposition of the Christian faith based on the Apostles' Creed. He emphasized the importance of scripture as well as God's sovereignty and concern for the individual. Even today scholars and students for the Presbyterian ministry study this work, which many consider the most important writing to come out of the Reformation. Calvin, however, wrote it because he considered it important that **everyone** from the king to the poorest commoner be informed about their faith. It was, if you like, the first Presbyterian communicants study guide.

This idea, that all members should understand their faith, has been a strong characteristic of Presbyterianism ever since. That Presbyterians require high academic requirements for members of their clergy also reflects this emphasis by John Calvin.

In the 1530s, William Farel, a fiery Swiss preacher, was leading the reform movement in Geneva, Switzerland. In 1536 he tried to persuade Calvin to join him in Geneva. Calvin did not want to go. He wished to pursue an academic life and to give himself to writing. He argued that physically he was too sickly, and emotionally too ill-tempered, to be a pastor to people.

The climax of the debate is recorded to have gone like this. "In the name of the Lord," cried Calvin, "have pity on me and let me serve God in some other way."

But Farel refused to take no as an answer. He replied to Calvin, "And I, in the name of Almighty God say to you: your studies are a mere excuse! If you refuse to dedicate yourself here with us to this work of God, God will curse you, for you seek yourself rather than Christ."

Calvin gave in and went to help establish the Reformation in Geneva. Some referred to him as the "Protestant Pope of Geneva" for what they viewed as his rather autocratic efforts to ensure that Geneva become a thoroughly Protestant city.

Of particular significance for Presbyterians in Canada was that, in Geneva, a refugee from Scotland came under Calvin's influence and tutelage. John Knox would eventually carry the reformed principles learned from Calvin back to Scotland. In turn, it would be the Church in Scotland, with both settlers and influence, which became formative in the early days of Presbyterianism in Canada.

In Geneva Calvin helped to organize this new Protestant city along the lines of the principles he had enunciated in the *Institutes*. Although many of Calvin's "reforms" would seem repressive and excessively legalistic by today's standards, he did initiate many enlightened policies. Safe haven was provided for refugees and hospitals were built for the aged and sick. As well, schools and universities were established.

Being of Reformed or Presbyterian persuasion does not mean we must slavishly follow everything John Calvin did or said. For example, he wore a large, broad-brimmed hat in church not because the Bible or faith demanded it but because in those days churches had pigeons. The long black Genevan gowns many Presbyterian ministers wear today were the usual dress worn in Calvin's time. He wore it during worship not as a religious symbol but because in those days church buildings were cold and draughty.

Still, there is much we can learn from him that will assist us in living out our faith.

A "this world" focus

When Cromwell said he would sooner meet a whole army with fixed bayonets than one Calvinist who believed he was doing God's will, it was another way of saying that the Reformed faith is "this worldly." It believes in involvement and change, not only in the lives of individuals, but in the structures of society.

Just before the federal election in Canada, in October 1993, I wrote an editorial in the *Presbyterian Record* entitled, "How Would John Calvin Vote in the Federal Election?" I pointed out that, although I might not be able to say specifically for which party Calvin would vote, I was convinced he would have taken an active part in the election. I pointed out that for Calvin there was no separation of church and state. Every part of the world was God's realm. Each had specific functions, derived from God.

Work or vocation also held an important place in Calvin's theology. He was concerned when people were unemployed. In

Geneva Calvin elicited state aid to establish new industries, such as the manufacture of cloth and watches, in order to provide employment for the refugees flooding into Geneva.

Some have claimed that Calvin was the father of modern day capitalism. These claims arise from Calvin's strong emphasis on the work ethic and his equally strong sense of stewardship. Although he exhibited a more positive view than most church leaders of his day to the emerging economic order of his time (capitalism), he would never have supported *laissez-faire* capitalism. Capitalism, yes, but capitalism with restraints. Interest on money loaned, but never exorbitant interest. And the benefits derived from the economic system should be shared: in Calvin's own words, "regulated by the law of love." Through the government, Calvin believed, you could love your neighbor in practical ways. Today, because the government has become so much a part of all our lives, it could be argued it is no longer possible to love your neighbor adequately without engaging in politics.

Calvin believed that all areas of life—political, social, and cultural—are spheres of God's action. I believe that for much of the 20th century The Presbyterian Church in Canada forgot or lost this emphasis of Calvin, as we will see when we come to consider the question of social involvement.

One lasting influence was Calvin's belief that the mind and reason were gifts of God to be cultivated and used in God's service. Today, as a part of that tradition, the Presbyterian Church continues to demand high educational standards for its ministers—a bachelor of arts degree followed by three or four years of study in theology.

For his part, John Knox was imbued by Calvin with a sense of the importance of education. Knox taught that in every community a school should be built along with a church. As a result, everywhere in the world it has gone, the Presbyterian church has established schools along with churches.

This was the case, for example, in Guyana. For many years The Presbyterian Church in Canada has carried out a mission there. Many of the schools were built and operated by the church. When the state was in a position to maintain an educational system, the Presbyterian Church happily handed over their schools to the state. Presbyterians possibly felt freer to do this than some other denominations because they believe the state is not solely a secular power but is also an instrument and acts at the will of God.

The emphasis on the mind and education has resulted in Presbyterianism producing more than its share of literary figures. Thomas McCulloch, an early Presbyterian minister in Nova Scotia, was described by Northrop Frye as the "founder of genuine Canadian humor." McCulloch had authored a number of anonymous letters in the newspaper, under the title *Letters of Mephibosheth Stepsure*, satirizing the morals and foibles of Nova Scotians. From the beginning of the First World War the two most popular novelists in Canada were Presbyterians. Lucy Maud Montgomery, the wife of a Presbyterian minister, wrote the still-popular *Anne of Green Gables* stories. Under the name of Ralph Connor, Presbyterian minister Charles Gordon wrote best sellers such as *Glengarry School Days* and *The Man From Glengarry*. In dramatic fashion, the stories recounted the efforts of Scots Presbyterian pioneers to recreate in Canada the strictly ordered society they had known in Scotland. More than three million copies of Connor's first three novels were sold around the world.

William Klempa, writing in 1994 on the Presbyterian contribution to the literary, political, and social life of Canada, recalls that the Rev. James McGregor came to Pictou, Nova Scotia, in 1786. He notes that McGregor's 44-year ministry and the lives of his descendants typify the Presbyterian contribution to Canada: "Among his direct descendants were four members of parliament, one lieutenant-governor, one judge, four professors and 11 teachers, four ministers, eight lawyers, two doctors, seven engineers, one artist, 15 merchants, eight nurses, and five authors."

The first Prime Minister of Canada, Sir John A. Macdonald, was a Presbyterian, describing himself as "a pillar of the church, albeit an outside pillar." Perhaps his reticence is reflected in the fact that in history he is better remembered for his drinking than for his religion.

A few years ago, a historical marker was unveiled on the lawn of the house next to Knox College in Toronto to commemorate the fact that Macdonald once lived there. To the shock of some, and the amusement of the students at Knox, when the covering was removed from the marker a large sign plastered over the official marker read, "Sir John A. Macdonald drank here."

What we believe

When we talk about what Reformed Christians believe, the first thing we must say is that, historically, they believe all those things about God and Jesus Christ that all Christians have believed. We often use the Apostles' Creed to reflect the core of what we hold in common with other Christians.

Persons joining a Presbyterian church are asked to affirm only those beliefs held in common by all Christian churches. We do not think it fair to ask any more of an ordinary member or in fact to ask more than Jesus himself required.

There are no prescribed or required questions that new members must answer when confessing their faith. For much of its history, persons wishing to become members of the Presbyterian Church were asked three questions, contained in the *Book of Common Order* (a book which contains various helps and orders for worship used by Presbyterian ministers on a voluntary basis).

The first question asked, "Do you confess your faith in God as your Heavenly Father, in Jesus Christ as Savior and Lord, and in the Holy Spirit as your sanctifier?" In more contemporary language it might read, "Do you put your trust in God as you would in a wise and loving parent; in Jesus who rescues you from the consequences of your sins, and whom you promise to follow as the final authority in your life; and in the Holy Spirit, God's presence in the world, who will be with you to work in your life to make you both holy and whole?"

The second question inquired, "Do you repent of your sins with a humble and contrite heart, and put your trust in the mercy of God which is in Christ Jesus?" In other words, "Do you feel badly enough about your sins to turn from them, and then rest your case and life in the generosity of God already displayed in the life of Jesus Christ?"

Finally, the question was asked, "Do you promise to make diligent use of the means of grace, and to be a faithful member of the church of God?" By assenting to this, new members promised to make regular use of the means God has provided to make his mercy, acceptance, and love real in their lives. These means include prayer, worship, the sacraments, Bible reading and study. To worship regularly with God's people, be faithful in sharing our material goods with others, and be involved in the pursuit of justice, both in our neighborhood and in the world, are aspects of what it means to be a faithful member of the church of God. In other words, you promise to pray, read and study your Bible, worship regularly, and give of your time, money, and talents to serve God.

In 1991, a new book called *The Book of Common Worship* was adopted for voluntary use by the church. The writers of this book tried to frame questions for those seeking membership in the church that reflected not only the best traditions in Presbyterianism but also what was happening in other denominations. In order to make clear the connection to baptism, the new book includes what we previously referred to as confirmation or joining the church within the baptismal service calling it "Baptism and Affirmation of Baptism." As you read the questions in this book you will see how they reflect much that is in the previous questions. After each question, the candidate is to reply with the words, "I do."

1. Trusting in the gracious mercy of God who has been faithful to us in all generations, do you turn away from sin, renounce evil and all powers in the world that rebel against God or oppose God's rule of justice and love?
2. Do you turn to Jesus Christ and offer your life to him as Lord and Savior?
3. Do you desire, in dependence on the power of the Holy Spirit, to mature as a Christian in the church, to seek the guidance of Christ as you listen for his Word, to celebrate his death and life at the table he provides, and to engage in his mission to the world?

After the congregation affirms its willingness to assist in the nurture and support of the new candidates, the minister will usually invite all present to confess their common faith by reciting The Apostles' Creed.

When you profess your faith it is likely you will be asked one or the other of these sets of questions. But it is also possible that other questions may be used. The important thing is that you will only be asked to profess what the whole church has traditionally believed to be necessary if you are to consider yourself a Christian.

But the Presbyterian Church expects much more of its leaders—ministers and ruling elders. The questions they are required to answer before ordination are prescribed by the church. Wherever you go, these questions will always be the same.

For a ruling elder they are as follows:

1. Do you believe in God the Father, made known in his son Jesus Christ our Lord, to whom the Holy Spirit witnesses in the Scriptures of the Old and New Testaments?
2. Do you accept the subordinate standards of this church and do you promise to be guided thereby in fostering Christian belief, worship, and service among the people?
3. Do you accept the government of this church by sessions, presbyteries, synods and general assemblies, and do you promise to share in and submit yourself to all lawful oversight therein, and to follow no divisive course but to seek the peace and unity of Christ among your people and throughout the Holy Catholic Church?
4. In accepting the office of elder, do you promise to perform your duties in the grace of the Lord Jesus Christ, striving to build up his Church and to strengthen her mission in the world?

For ministers the following question is substituted for the fourth one above:

> Do you promise in the strength and grace of the Lord Jesus Christ to conduct yourself in your private and public life as becomes his gospel, and do you give yourself diligently and cheerfully to the service of Christ's word, sacraments and discipline, for the furtherance of his reconciling mission in the world?

Ministers and ruling elders are expected to know something about and be committed to some of the distinctive beliefs and emphases of the Reformed and Presbyterian faith. Many of these are contained in what we call our subordinate standards, referred to in the questions put to candidates when they are ordained or installed as an elder. By subordinate we mean subordinate to the Bible which is the primary standard to guide our faith and life. The Presbyterian Church in Canada has two subordinate standards.

The Westminster Confession

The first is the *Westminster Confession of Faith.* This document has guided most of the Presbyterian churches in the English-speaking world. An assembly authorized by the English parliament created this document during sessions held between 1643 and 1646 in Westminster Abbey. Most of the authors of this document were Presbyterians. The parliament hoped that adopting a single confession of faith would assist in promoting unity in the nation. Unfortunately for them, the church in England did not adopt this confession. But the Church of Scotland did and so it was passed on to The Presbyterian Church in Canada.

The *Westminster Confession* seeks to lay out in a systematic and ordered way the Reformed perspective on the faith. It contains 35 chapters beginning with chapter one on the Holy Scripture, and ending with a chapter on the Last Judgment. In between are chapters on the Trinity and predestination, as well as one on marriage and divorce, and the duty of the civil magistrate. By the way, the confession's views on divorce are more generous than those of some churches today, even in 1646 providing for the possibility of failed marriage and the remarriage of divorced persons. In conformity to the Presbyterian view of the Bible, each phrase in the confession is referenced to scriptural passages.

When studying the *Westminster Confession* we should remember that it was written in the 17th century in a pre-scientific era. The confession also reflects a time when Protestants and Roman Catholics were hostile to each other, and before much of modern scholarship, which has illumined the Bible in modern times, had taken place. That is why elders, although they are asked to accept the subordinate standards, do so only "under the continual illumination and correction of the Holy Spirit speaking in the Scriptures." This means that the Holy Spirit speaking through the Bible always takes precedence over all confessions, including the *Westminster Confession*.

For the sake of easier learning, the main tenants of the confession were laid out in question-and-answer form in two versions: the Larger and the Shorter Catechism. Yes, the Larger Catechism is **much** larger.

When I was a child growing up in a Presbyterian church school much emphasis was placed on learning the catechism by memory. Those who correctly responded to the 107 questions, asked in two or three sessions, were awarded a handsome certificate. Although successful in this endeavor 40 years ago, today I can only readily recall the first question and answer. But knowing that question and answer makes the whole effort worthwhile, for seldom has so brief a statement encapsulated the Reformed faith so well:

Q: What is man's chief end?

A: Man's chief end is to glorify God, and to enjoy him forever.

This tradition in our church of using catechisms for learning the faith goes back to John Calvin. In 1541 he wrote a catechism for children which was used in the Reformed Church in Switzerland, as well as in churches in many other countries. Every Sunday, parts of it were used in the church service so that the whole catechism would be covered once every year. Children had to come forward regularly to the minister to be examined in the catechism.

It is possible that 100 years ago, if you were a child growing up in a Presbyterian family on a farm in Canada, each night at the supper table your father would lead in family worship. (Source: Jean Stewart in *The Believers*.) He would read from the Bible and pray. You, your brother and sister would also be expected to pray.

Sunday morning, if you were eight or nine, you would be called to recite the catechism, one or two questions at a time. Older brothers and sisters would be going through it for a second or third time.

During Sunday worship the minister would announce where he would visit that week. If it was your house on Wednesday your mother would make elaborate preparations for his visit. When he arrived your father would come in from the fields. When you arrived home from school you would join the family in the not-often-used parlor. The minister would lead the family in Bible reading and prayer and then call upon you to answer some of the questions from the catechism you had been studying.

After this ordeal all would retire to the kitchen for a meal together.

In 1991, after the fall of the Soviet Union, I saw some of this tradition still alive in the Presbyterian (Reformed) churches in the Ukraine. I went to visit the Ukraine with the Moderator of our church.

Because of communism, the churches there had been cut off from contact with the churches in the West for many years. As a result, many of them did things which we would consider old-fashioned. For example, many sing without the assistance of a musical instrument. In some churches the men sit on one side and the women on the other. And, of course, there are no women ministers or elders.

We visited on Ascension Day, which happened to coincide with the Russian holiday called Freedom Day. While many paraded to the Lenin monument to extol the virtues of communism, Christians gathered in their churches for worship. The church was beginning to experience a new freedom and this was the first occasion in 40 years that the state had allowed the church to accept young people into membership.

Needless to say it was a very emotional event. Many tears were shed, including some by the Moderator and myself, although we could not understand a word of what was being said. In one congregation about 100 young people were received into membership. Before being received, each was asked to stand and to answer one or two questions from the catechism. In preparation for membership they had memorized the whole of the catechism and, without knowing what question might be asked, responded easily and perfectly.

Today, in our own church, less emphasis is placed upon learning the catechism. However, the church still believes it is important that we continue to study the Christian faith throughout our lives. When the minister visits, he or she is unlikely to ask you a question from the Shorter Catechism. But ministers still move throughout the congregation teaching the scriptures and praying with the people.

As well, nearly every Presbyterian congregation today provides a church school with educational opportunities for everyone from small children to adults.

Concerning church and nation...

When our church adopted the *Westminster Confession* as its subordinate standard in 1875, chapter 23, which dealt with the civil magistrate, became a problem because of differing views in the church about the proper relationship between church and state. A compromise was reached by which the uniting churches agreed that nothing in the *Westminster Confession* or either catechism regarding the power and duty of the civil magistrate "shall be held to sanction any principle or view inconsistent with full liberty of conscience in matters of religion." This was, historian John Moir comments, a peculiarly Canadian formula which basically said that "the headship of Christ simply means whatever you want it to mean."

Most Presbyterians happily went along with this until the Second World War. In 1955 the General Assembly adopted a *Declaration of Faith Concerning Church and Nation* as our second subordinate standard. But the process of its adoption had been long and difficult, beginning in 1942 with a petition from the Presbytery of Paris in Ontario and culminating in the declaration's acceptance, after many revisions, 13 years later.

The declaration begins by affirming the headship of Christ over both church and state. It follows this affirmation with a description of the relation and duties each has to the other, the question of power and its use, and the responsibility of the church to resist tyranny. This document significantly influenced the modern development of the Presbyterian Church, especially in its willingness to begin to grapple seriously with social issues.

As a Reformed church, we must always take seriously the task of reformulating the faith in creeds and confessions which speak to the contemporary situation. Presbyterians have always taken this task with utmost seriousness. This is what is meant when we say we are a confessional church. We believe it important to confess or state in a clear and rational way what we believe about our faith.

Living Faith

An event of great importance happened in our church when, in 1984, the General Assembly accepted a document called *Living Faith* and commended it to the church as an acceptable statement of faith, useful for both worship and study. At that time the framers of the document did not ask that it immediately become a part of our subordinate standards. First, they believed it must be tried and tested in the church. Since its publication, this statement has become tremendously popular in our church. Often you will find it in the pews of the church. Frequently parts of it will be used during worship, similar to the way the catechism was used in the past, as an expression of the congregation's faith.

The Committee on Church Doctrine labored over it for many years before producing the final copy. Although we have said the task of reformulating the faith is an important one, it is not easy to obtain a consensus in the church as to what such a confession should say. In fact, the Committee on Church Doctrine had been working many years trying to come up with a suitable contemporary confession. A number of their previous efforts had been rejected by the church.

Finally, a member of the committee, Stephen Hayes, then minister of St. Andrew's Church in Cobourg, Ontario, proposed that the committee use for inspiration and as a general outline a confession produced by the Presbyterian Church in the United States called *A Declaration of Faith*. Although warned by several experts that this was not the traditional way one produced a confession and that it was likely to be unsuccessful, Stephen and the committee persevered through many revisions until it gained acceptance by the church.

Although it has not yet been accepted as a subordinate standard of our church, its wide acceptance and use will soon result, I believe, in this happening.

One of the attractive features of this document is that it is written in free verse which makes it particularly useful for worship. I believe every Canadian Presbyterian should own a copy of *Living Faith: A Statement of Christian Belief.*

Let me give you a small taste of what it is like by quoting a paragraph from the section entitled, "God the Holy Spirit:"

> The Holy Spirit accompanies us on our journey of faith.
> We may not always be sure of this presence.
> Yet God's Spirit is with us,
> sometimes gently, sometimes powerfully,
> guiding us in the midst of life,
> our comfort and our help.
> Christian life is pilgrimage:

it begins, continues, and ends in God.

To be true to our tradition, this confession contains extensive scriptural references to all parts of the statement as well as cross-references to other reformed and ecumenical creeds and confessions.

Particularly Presbyterian

Many of the main beliefs of Presbyterians are held in common with Christians in other denominations. But some beliefs or doctrines have come to be particularly associated with Presbyterianism. Many of these go back to what John Calvin taught and believed at the time of the Reformation.

Some people believe that Presbyterians hold a picture of God which is excessively cold and austere, more informed by the Old Testament than the New. They believe this was the picture of God Calvin painted, that before the arrival of Calvin, God was a benevolent, kindly sort of God. But in Calvin's hands God was transformed into a hard, demanding, and unfeeling deity—a God whose chief function was to prevent people having fun. Some of Calvin's enemies in Geneva coined this phrase: "Better with Beza in hell than with Calvin in Heaven!" Beza was Calvin's successor in Geneva who reversed some of Calvin's teaching, particularly in regard to resisting tyrants.

The idea that Calvin and Calvinists are antifun continues to surface in popular literature and discourse. Recently, researcher Gerald Klerman coined the phrase "pharmacological Calvinism." The term refers to "a general distrust of drugs used for nontherapeutic purposes and a general conviction that if a drug makes you feel good, it must be morally bad."

Even television evangelist Jimmy Swaggart got into the act. "Calvin," he was quoted as saying, "has, I believe, caused untold millions of souls to be damned..." That comment would have shocked Calvin. He always carefully maintained that people's ultimate destiny lay in the hands of God alone.

An exception to this tendency to caricature Presbyterians is the movie *A River Runs Through It.* The film paints a fair and honest picture of what Presbyterianism is really like. Robert Redford sensitively tells the story of Presbyterian minister John Maclean and his two sons, and fly fishing. An early line catches our attention and sets the tone for the picture: "In our family there was no clear line between religion and fly fishing." Right. That's the way life is meant to operate. Presbyterians are called to glorify and enjoy God in everything they do.

Predestination

Part of this caricature of Presbyterianism comes from Calvin's association with the belief called predestination, the idea that God, through foreknowledge, ordains some (the elect) to be saved.

You may have heard the story of the elderly Presbyterian lady who was asked if she was saved. "O yes," she replied. "And how long ago?" her questioner persisted. "I reckon about three million years ago," she replied. "Three million years ago!" exclaimed the astonished questioner. "O yes," she said. "Before the foundations of the world God chose me as one of God's own."

To say that God chose **some** begs the question as to whether or not God foreordained the rest to eternal damnation. The belief that God did both is referred to as double predestination. Presbyterians are always in danger of falling into this error. Even Scottish poet Robert Burns did. In *Holy Willie's prayer* he speaks of a God who, "Sends one to Heaven an' ten to Hell/ a' for Thy Glory!"

Sometimes the themes of hell and damnation or the threat of them have played too prominent a role in Presbyterianism. Some even claim that Presbyterians come to actually enjoy it. They feel a worship service is not complete without the reminder that they are miserable sinners in danger of damnation.

Stephen Leacock picked up this theme in his story of "The Rival Churches of St. Asaph and St. Osoph." (In *Arcadian Adventures with the Idle Rich*, McClelland & Stewart, 1959.) When the Presbyterian church, St. Osoph, inducts a new minister, Rev. Uttermust Dumfarthing, he preaches his first sermon on eternal punishment. He tells the congregation he is convinced 70 percent of them are destined for hell. "The congregation was so swelled next Sunday that the minister raised the percentage to 85, and everyone went away delighted."

I admit I have noticed that on those occasions when ministers work themselves into a lather about the sins of the congregation so that they are barely able to stagger to the door to greet the congregation at the end of the service, they will often be greeted by the words: "What a delightful talk you gave this morning, Reverend."

But the belief in predestination did not, as some suppose, originate in the mind of Calvin. It lies deeply embedded in scripture itself. In Romans 8:29–30, Saint Paul declares that, "For those whom God foreknew were also predestined to be conformed to the image of God's Child, in order that Christ might be the firstborn among many believers. And those whom God predestined, God also called; and those whom God called, God also justified; and those whom God justified, God also glorified." (*An Inclusive Language Lectionary*)

And Calvin was always reluctant, more reluctant I might add than many of his followers since then, to propound the belief in double predestination. His hesitancy lay in the reluctance he saw in scripture itself.

Unlike some of his followers since, Calvin seldom used this doctrine to terrorize people, or as someone put it, "to scare hell out of them in order to get them to heaven." Rather, Calvin saw this doctrine primarily as a comfort and encouragement to believers.

In the chaos of life there is a plan. Life does not simply go around in circles as the Greeks claimed. Life is not a hit and miss or accidental affair. It has a beginning, a middle, and an end. In this journey, God is supreme; the world's leaders, though powerful, are not. As long as God is sovereign, neither the people nor the state can assume such a role.

"The great point," wrote Calvin in the *Institutes* "is that we who are consecrated and dedicated to God should not henceforth think or speak, design or act without a view to his glory."

Overarching all of this is Presbyterianism's emphasis on God's sovereignty. Simply put this means that God created everything. All of creation depends upon God, never the reverse. God stands above, beyond, and over the creation. God is creator; we are God's creations. As such we may reflect God, but we are not an extension of God. God is separate from the creation. We do not have a spark of immortality within us. When we die, we really die and must depend on God to raise us from the dead if we are to live again.

The fact that God is sovereign does not mean God remains

untouched by what happens on earth. God proved that through God's love shown to us in the life, death, and resurrection of Jesus Christ. Through God's spirit, we say the Holy Spirit, God actively engages the world in every aspect of life—personal, cultural, political, and industrial.

When it comes to what Presbyterians believe about sin the phrase "total depravity" often pops up. Actually, this sounds a lot worse than it really is. Basically, it means that every action or part of our life is touched or influenced by sin. It doesn't mean we never do anything honorable or good. But like the salt we add to our potatoes, or cream which diffuses through our coffee and influences the whole cup, sin influences every part of our existence. All have rebelled against God and transgressed God's will for their lives. The operative thing here is not individual sin, but our sinful condition from which none are exempt.

Sometimes Presbyterians emphasize sin to the exclusion of the forgiveness and freedom God gives us. On the other hand, not to face the power and reality of sin, Presbyterians claim, is to live in an unreal world; it is to live in an even more dangerous world.

Charles Colson, who worked for President Nixon and ended up in jail as a result of the Watergate scandal, makes the same point. He said he did everything to avoid the appearance of conflict of interest. He felt confident he would always do right. But, as he points out, he ended up in jail. Why? "Because," he says, "we are never more dangerous than when we are feeling self-righteous."

This situation is not something we can overcome by ourselves, by working or trying harder. We cannot pull ourselves up by our own bootstraps. It requires outside intervention. Only God can help (save) us.

None of this is to say that non-Christians never do any good. It simply recognizes that all of our thoughts, words, and deeds are affected by sin. And this influence of sin will never be completely eliminated in this life.

Karl Menninger, a famous psychiatrist, wrote a book entitled *Whatever Happened to Sin?* In it he warns about the modern attempt to eliminate sin from our vocabulary by calling it by some lesser name. We have transformed "sin" into a "crime," a "symptom," an "illness," and a "collective irresponsibility." At one time, he says, sin was "an ominous and serious word." To use the word today is to be old-fashioned. With the disappearance of the word has also gone the notion of "the allocation of responsibility for evil." There are no bad children, only bad parents or grandparents. Yet sin, as a reality, is still with us and in us. But today, because of this evolution, we are less able to deal with it. Perhaps it is not accidental that Karl Menninger was a Presbyterian.

Presbyterians believe that only one thing remains stronger than sin—God's grace.

A few years ago I hired a young woman to work in my office. Her previous experience had been almost exclusively in the Baptist church. After a while she said to me, "You know there is one word which turns up more that any other in what Presbyterians write. That word is grace. It must be the central tenet of Presbyterian faith."

I could only reply to her that I hoped and prayed she was right. Presbyterians believe their acceptance by God is based on God's unmerited and undeserved love towards us (grace). We believe we have been called to share this good news about God with the whole creation.

I said at the beginning of this chapter that reformed faith has the capacity to form remarkable people. Sometimes this can be seen with great clarity in the life of a person. Such is the case of Nell Dickey.

In 1974, her daughter, a student at Erindale College in Mississauga, Ontario, was viciously murdered. Three years later, Charles Williams was convicted of her murder and that of another young woman. In 1984, 10 years after his conviction, Williams began receiving day passes from prison. *The Toronto Sun* wrote a story based largely on interviews done with the mothers of the girls who had been murdered. Mrs. Dickey, in what I consider a remarkable and grace-filled statement, said she remained opposed to capital punishment despite her daughter's murder. "Ultimate decisions about people's lives," she said, "should be left in the hands of God." And the parole board. Yes, as human instruments courts and parole boards sometimes make mistakes. We all do. But she was still prepared to believe it too was an instrument of God to do God's work in the world.

Chapter 4

Photo: *Presbyterian Record*

1994 General Assembly.

Family discipline: how God governs the Presbyterian Church

> A great Presbyterian ideal...is that the people, the whole people, and not the clergy or officials, are the church; that ministers are not a class apart, vested with special rights and powers, but simply members of the church, set apart to serve in the church, while other members of the church, engaged in other callings, provide for their needs in that service, and thus the work of the church is shared alike by all.
>
> —Ephraim Scott addressing the General Assembly in 1925

Part of the reason I am a Presbyterian today is because of church government. As I mentioned in chapter one, I was 10 when my parents decided to move back to their hometown. Logic suggested we would attend the Baptist church in which my mother had been brought up. My parents decided against this, however, due to a particularly difficult time the local Baptist church was experiencing in those days. Instead, they decided we would attend the Presbyterian church as a temporary measure until the latest skirmish ended and we could return to being Baptists as God intended us to be.

Because, in the Baptist system, pastors can be removed by the vote of the congregation, the Baptist congregation in my parents' hometown attempted to deal with their conflict through an annual vote to remove their pastor. But this yearly sacrifice of the pastor never solved the deeper problems of this congregation. And because this went on for several years we never left the Presbyterian church.

In the Presbyterian system, a congregation cannot remove their pastor in this way. This power is vested in the presbytery. Members of a congregation can complain to the presbytery about their minister, but it is only by presbytery action that a minister can be removed. This affords the minister some protection from frivolous complaints or actions by members of the congregation.

First encounters

After I was ordained and became a minister myself, I began attending the General Assembly (the highest court of our church) every few years when my turn came up. Under normal circumstances that happens every six years. The clerk of the Assembly, who carries out many of the same functions as a secretary in other organizations, was at that time a colorful character in the national church by the name of Louis Fowler. Frequently, members of the Assembly would call upon him to offer rulings, especially in disputes over proper procedure. Often he would refer to something in the *Book of Forms* (a book which contains a summation of the rules and procedures of the church collected over many years). I studied this book in seminary and felt I had a pretty good knowledge of what it contained. But sometimes, when pressed to give the authority for his ruling, Fowler would simply shout "wont and usage." That seemed to have the effect of ending most arguments. But it confused me. I did not wish to display either my ignorance or lack of education by asking what he meant. Was it a rule of the church I had somehow missed? Eventually, it dawned on me. Fowler meant exactly what he said. When he cried "wont and usage" it meant there was no rule written down to cover this specific situation, but this was the way we usually dealt with it in the past (usage), and this was the most effective way of dealing with it now (wont).

Two other aspects of Presbyterian Church government make it particularly confusing for newcomers. We refer to the various bodies which govern Presbyterians as courts. But they are not really courts like we normally think of courts—forums which receive evidence and make judgments in particular cases. (Although Presbyterian courts sometimes do have this function, as you will see by a later example.) Most of the time and effort of church courts is taken up by issues of Christian education, mission, and social action and justice issues.

The other confusing aspect for newcomers is the language that we use in church courts. If you have ever returned from a medical appointment complaining that your doctor speaks another language, you will have some idea what I mean. Archaic words like *sederent* (which means that particular session or meeting), or *in seriatim* (which means you deal with issues one after another, in order), tend to confuse the uninitiated.

After the 1994 Assembly, Mark Tremblay attempted, in a humorous way, to make this point by writing to the *Record.* In part his letter read, "I want to examine *cum nota* some of our language *seriatim, anent* its archaic character. I do so *ex parte*, with no apology for the other side. I make *bona fide* proposals *apud acta*... I offer some proposals in *hunc effectum*, not *de facto* but rather *simpliciter*..." He concludes: "Of course, my *ad hoc* committee of one shall be judged to have acted *ultra vires, de jure*. Submitted *simpliciter*, but respectfully."

Many of us believe there are no good reasons for adding an unnecessary degree of confusion to an already confusing situation by using ancient words and terminology. I'm happy to report a move is underway to update the language we use.

Even without the language barrier, your first encounter with the government of the church may have been as confusing as mine. I hope this chapter may unravel some of the mysteries of how God directs the deliberations and the decisions of our church.

Christ—the head of the church

Presbyterians like to begin any discussion of this subject with words that are spoken before the questions are asked at an ordination: "Jesus Christ is the only King and head of the Church." So when we talk about church government we are really talking about how we believe God orders our life and faith in the church on earth.

Presbyterians believe that a glimpse of the way God leads the church can be seen in the Old and New Testaments. We do not argue that our way is the only way, nor that portions of other systems cannot also be seen in the Bible. We simply want to affirm that we believe the system we use is based upon and agreeable to scripture, and over time has been found effective.

Every denomination has some kind of structure or order. Basically there are three kinds. The congregational form of church government, found among Baptists for example, gives most power into the hands of independent and autonomous congregations. In the Episcopal form of government, seen in Anglican and Roman Catholic denominations, authority resides primarily in a hierarchy of ordained individuals. This authority is passed on from one bishop to the next in what is believed to be an unbroken succession going back to the time of the apostles. Sometimes this is referred to as apostolic succession. In the Presbyterian form of government, this authority to rule resides in a series of church courts. Through these bodies, Presbyterians believe the church acts to choose and authorize men and women for ministry. Rather than being ordained to an office, Presbyterians only ordain after the person has received a call to a congregation, mission, or other ministry.

Representative government

Presbyterianism is a representative form of government based on the selection of elders. Elders are spoken of both in Israel and in Jewish communities at the time of Christ. In the Book of Acts we find the following: "And when they had appointed elders for them in every church, with prayer and fasting they committed them to the Lord in whom they believed." (Acts 14:23) In the first chapter of Titus, Paul lays down the qualities an elder should have. These include being hospitable, prudent, upright, devout, and self-controlled. The elder must also love goodness.

The word elder comes from the Greek word *presbuteros*, from which we derive our name, Presbyterian—meaning those who are ruled by elders. In the New Testament, elders seemed to have very similar functions to bishops. In fact, some would argue that the two words were interchangeable.

Since the time of Calvin, some elders have been trained to preach and teach. We usually refer to them as ministers, pastors, or teaching elders. Others have been trained as ruling elders or lay leaders who share with the minister in the leadership of the church.

This idea of an equal and shared leadership between the two kinds of elders in the Presbyterian Church is an important principle adhered to in all the courts of the church, with the exception of the local congregation which usually has only one or two ministers. In all the other courts you will find an equal number of ruling elders and ministers.

So how does all of this work in practical terms?

The session

Each local congregation elects a group of elders who meet in what is called a session. The session has the overall responsibility for the direction, Christian education, and pastoral care of the congregation. Each elder will have a district, a group of inividuals and families assigned to his or her care. The elder's responsibility is to keep in touch with these people, ministering to their needs and bringing any of their concerns to the attention of the session.

Any man or woman 21 years of age or older may be elected as an elder. When elected, they are ordained or set apart for this work by the session, an ordination that lasts for life although there may be times when they may request a leave of absence from their duties. If elders move to a new congregation, they remain elders, but cannot act in that congregation unless the congregation elects them to the session.

Most Presbyterian congregations also have a board of managers. They are elected by the congregation and are charged with administrating its financial affairs. In a sense, they are a committee of the congregation, the financial committee, if you like. One-third of the board are elected each year for a three-year term.

Because of the division of responsibilities in the congregation between the session and the board, often you find tensions arising between the two groups. The board will often feel they have the "dirty jobs" to do, such as paying the bills and maintaining the property. They view the session as sitting in splendid isolation, making the real decisions affecting the congregation's life without regard to reality.

As a result, some congregations have gone to a unified system where all committees of the congregation include members both of the session and the board. As a minimum, it is always wise to have regular joint meetings and/or representatives of the session on the board. Then, at least, the board will feel the session has some understanding of the problems they face.

But it remains true that the ultimate power resides with the session. They are the ones who will be held responsible for whatever happens in the congregation by the higher courts.

The presbytery

The court to which the session is responsible is called a presbytery. This is usually a geographical area composed of a number of Presbyterian congregations. Presently, there are 45 presbyteries from Newfoundland to British Columbia. The minister of each congregation plus one ruling elder, chosen by the session and called the representative elder, attend the presbytery. Presbytery meets anywhere from a few times each year, to monthly.

The presbytery makes extremely important decisions affecting the congregations. The presbytery occupies the position in the Presbyterian Church which Anglicans and Roman Catholics reserve for their bishops. Who will be ordained, and the ordinations themselves, are decided by the presbytery. And although congregations have the freedom to go out and search for a new minister when they need one, the call to that minister must be approved by both the presbytery to which and from which the minister is called before he or she begins work in the new congregation. Matters of discipline regarding ministers fall to the presbytery, as do all decisions about church property.

Presbyteries have the responsibility to establish new congregations within their bounds. Often they will provide educational training events, and sometimes they make pronouncements regarding issues which affect their congregations and members.

The synod

The next court, called the synod, is composed of several presbyteries. All the members of the presbyteries attend the annual synod meeting. Today in Canada, the Presbyterian Church has eight synods based roughly, but not always, on provincial boundaries. Some people think synods are an extra layer of government in our system, much like the Senate in the federal government, which some feel we no longer need. Others, particularly in more remote areas of Canada, find the once-a-year meeting of the synod a useful time of fellowship and renewal.

William Allen, the minister of the Presbyterian church in Kitimat, British Columbia, tells of the typical difficulties in getting to the yearly synod meeting in Vancouver. The story begins with him waiting for the regularly scheduled plane from Kitimat to Vancouver. What could be simpler? Right?

The airport speaker announces the flight has been cancelled. But all is not lost. The passengers will receive a bus ride to Prince Rupert and from there a midnight flight to Vancouver. At 1:30 in the morning the synod hospitality committee rescues him at the airport. A short time later he crawls into bed in a hotel room in White Rock hoping not to waken his roommate. The delay, he notes, means he has missed the Friday night sessions and a chance to socialize with friends not seen for a year.

For many, such as William Allen, who minister in isolated areas, the synod can provide a much-needed time of renewal. With this in mind, many synods now build into their agenda a period of study and reflection. Most of the church camps across Canada are operated by the synods. Sometimes a synod will deal with an appeal against some action of a presbytery, but most of these go directly to the highest or supreme court of the church which is called the General Assembly.

The General Assembly

The General Assembly meets annually the first week in June. The location of the meeting varies from year to year.

In 1994, the Assembly met on the campus of the University of

Toronto and was hosted by Knox College as part of their 150th anniversary celebrations. The opening worship service drew together almost 1,000 Presbyterians. The huge organ in Convocation Hall lifted the hymns in a way most Presbyterians have never experienced. Adding to the enjoyment was the 50-voice choir from the local East Toronto Korean Church. Following an address by the past Moderator, a new Moderator was elected and installed. The evening concluded with the whole gathering celebrating the Lord's Supper together. You can imagine the inspiration and excitement that such a service provides for many who may never have worshiped with more than 100 Presbyterian brothers and sisters at any one time.

Those who attend these meetings, one-sixth of the ministers and ruling elders of all the presbyteries, are referred to as commissioners. They are usually chosen by rotation, although a presbytery is free to send whomever they choose. For example, if one of their number has been nominated as Moderator, it becomes essential that this person be a commissioner to the Assembly. Each commissioner bears a responsibility, or commission, to rule with wisdom and integrity, and is expected to report on their stewardship to the presbytery when they return from General Assembly.

Most of the time of this court is taken up with hearing reports and giving direction to the various boards and committees of the church. The decisions of the General Assembly are final. It is the court of last appeal.

Of course it is possible for an Assembly to make a decision one year, which a succeeding Assembly may reverse in a following year. For many years, our church supported the right of the state to put to death someone who took the life of another person. Eventually, the church decided, through the General Assembly, that it could no longer support capital punishment and it made a statement to this effect.

Like all other courts, with the exception of the session where the minister automatically becomes the moderator (chairperson), the General Assembly chooses one of its own number to act as Moderator. The Moderator is elected primarily to preside over the General Assembly for the week it is in session. Practically, for the year following, the Moderator serves a ceremonial and inspirational role,

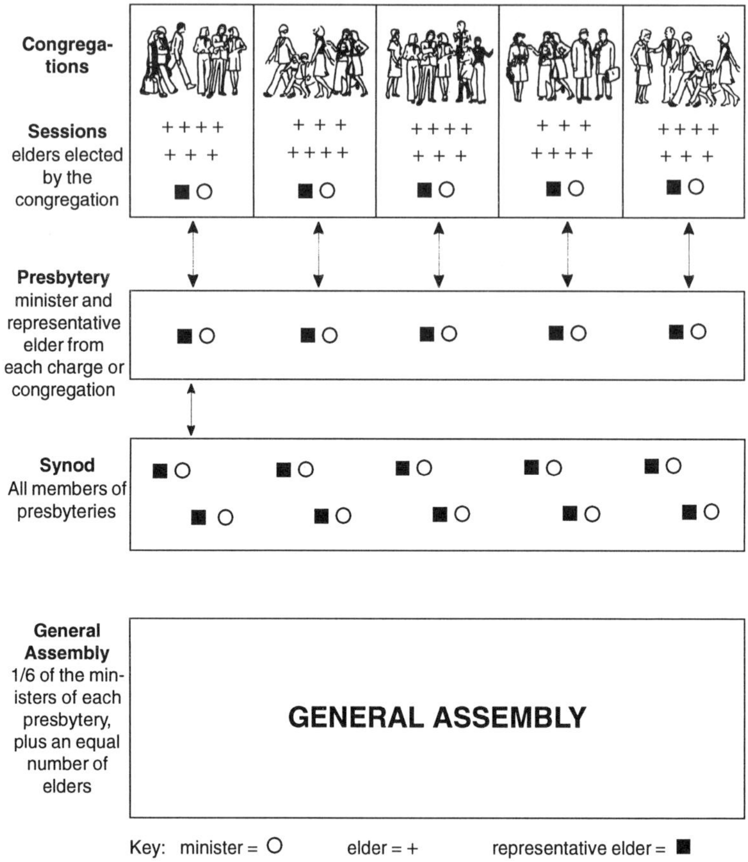

traveling throughout the church and often making an overseas trip to visit partner churches or missionaries in the field.

First-time commissioners to General Assembly often find the business and the rules governing it confusing. Meeting missionaries and visitors from partner churches from around the world often becomes their most vivid and lasting memory. Most leave the Assembly impressed by the wide-ranging concerns of the church, the commitment of her leaders, and their role in decision-making.

Problem solving

But how does this work for the ordinary persons in the pew who may have concerns or grievances? They must first take them to the session. If they do not find a satisfactory resolution there, they may take their concern to the presbytery, and then either on to the synod or General Assembly. As I have already said, once the General Assembly has made a decision the case becomes closed. Some complain that the system is slow and cumbersome. Others argue that justice must always be slow.

All of the courts and elders operate under a book of rules called the *Book of Forms*. Some of the rules in this book go back as far as the *Second Book of Discipline*. This document was adopted by the General Assembly in Scotland in 1581 to guide the Scottish church in matters of church organization and the conduct of its life after the Reformation. Other rules in the *Book of Forms* were made and passed as recently as the last General Assembly.

For example, here's a rule, still in force, which goes back to the *Second Book of Discipline*: "Every court, except the session, must (and the session may), before its rising, determine the time and place of its next meeting, and intimate this publicly." If you were to visit one of the courts of the church (all are open to visitors except sessions), you would see the moderator rise at the end of the business and just before pronouncing the benediction he or she would announce, "This court now stands adjourned to meet again on such and such date and time at such and such place." Moderators have done that continuously in the Presbyterian Church since 1578.

Each year the General Assembly makes decisions about adding, deleting, or modifying rules in the *Book of Forms*. For example, in 1985, the General Assembly passed this rule regarding elders: "Elders continue elders for life unless deposed or suspended in process of discipline. Nevertheless they may demit [resign] the active exercise of the office in any particular congregation." After the Assembly, this rule was then added to the *Book of Forms*.

In 1994, the Assembly decided that ministers who undertake pastoral services (for example, weddings, baptisms, funerals) in a congregation other than their own will be required to consult with and receive permission in writing from the local congregation.

If an Assembly passes a rule which will change the present law of the church, it must submit it to the presbyteries and the majority of the presbyteries must agree to it before it becomes a part of the law of the church. This was the case with the last example I gave.

In other words, the *Book of Forms* is a living and constantly changing book. Just as Presbyterians believe the law, such as that embodied in the Ten Commandments, has been given to us by a gracious God for our betterment, so we believe the law of the church is a gift of God to get us from A to B in the most helpful and efficient manner.

After so many years you might imagine that the *Book of Forms* has grown to several volumes. The new revised edition produced in 1993 contains only 150 pages and that includes the table of contents and an exhaustive index. So although people sometimes complain that the laws of the church are becoming as convoluted and numerous as the laws of the country, that is really not the case.

Like any good gift, the law too can be distorted. It can be turned into a form of legalism for which it was not intended, or distorted and used for wrong ends. We have all witnessed those who seek to use it for their own ends or as a way of attacking others. Some will attempt to use it to stall the clear will of the majority in the court.

In the 1960s, I served a congregation in the Presbytery of Hamilton. The presbytery debated the issue of the ordination of women. Clearly, the decision would ultimately be in favor of ordination. But those who were opposed used every means available to put off or stall the decision. More recently, when the report on human sexuality was under debate by the General Assembly, those opposed to it tried every means in church law to prevent it from being adopted. And they did so despite the fact that the overwhelming majority of the commissioners favored it.

Of course, church courts are not infallible. Sometimes they can be wrong. For many years our church did not allow women to serve as ruling elders and ministers. Gradually we came to see that this was wrong. When that happened, the *Book of Forms* was modified to reflect the mind of the church.

Let's see how all of this might work in a specific case. Here is a fictitious story about a real problem. It illustrates how, in the past, the courts have addressed such problems.

The Presbytery of the Lake receives a petition from St. Andrew's, a large, downtown, city church requesting assistance in resolving a dispute between some of the members of the congregation and their minister. Pastor Bill is a man of great eloquence. He is popular throughout the community. However, he has become involved in the charismatic (speaking in tongues) movement, and this, together with differences over his style of ministry, has brought him into dispute with some members and elders. Some simply do not like his "new ideas" while others feel he acts unilaterally without consulting the session.

The presbytery, in good Presbyterian fashion, appointed a committee to meet with all parties involved. In the end they concluded that Pastor Bill had lost the confidence of his people and should resign. When he refused to do this, the presbytery removed him as minister of St. Andrew's.

Pastor Bill refused to accept this decision and appealed the decision to General Assembly. The Assembly appointed a judicial commission. Once again it met with all parties involved and after carefully weighing the evidence it concurred with the decision of the presbytery.

Again refusing to accept this decision, Pastor Bill, still a minister of the Presbyterian Church, took a large number of elders and members from his previous congregation and established a new congregation. The commission of the General Assembly appealed to Pastor Bill to reconsider this action. When he refused they removed him as a minister of The Presbyterian Church in Canada.

Over the years, Pastor Bill served with various independent missions and causes. In the end this fictitious story had a happy ending. Pastor Bill eventually applied for and was reinstated as a minister of The Presbyterian Church in Canada. He eventually retired and is now an active participant in the life of the Presbytery of the Lake which had originally removed him from his congregation. It took 20 years, but healing finally came.

In the vast majority of cases a solution is found much quicker than the example I have offered. Most do not find it necessary to appeal from one court to the next. Presbyterians generally are amenable to the decisions made by the various courts of the church.

No one has ever claimed the Presbyterian system moves quickly but most find that it moves with justice and with openness to the leading of God's spirit.

Chapter 5

Photo: *Presbyterian Record*

Knox Presbyterian Church
Bluevale, Ontario.

Photo: *Presbyterian Record*

Bluevale United Church
Bluevale, Ontario.

Other relatives: one church

> ...the purpose of the ecumenical movement is to express more fully, effectively, and visibly in the world, the unity which the church has, and always has had, by the action of God.
>
> —Eoin Mackay, Presbyterian minister, former president of the Canadian Council of Churches

Several Christmases ago a member of my congregation gave all the members of the church a gift. She wrote a play for our Christmas pageant. Along with the traditional elements, she included a part by which various members came to the front of the sanctuary and offered their gifts. In preparation for this, the nativity story was told in terms of gift giving.

As each person was mentioned, they came and took their place in the drama unfolding before the congegation. After Joseph and Mary had taken their place, we awaited the arrival of the baby

Jesus. Two small girls, one black and the other white, had been chosen to carry in the baby Jesus. Both took their task with great seriousness, but both became increasingly agitated with the progress and care of the other. On the chancel steps they started to fight over Jesus. Mary had to leave her place in the stable to rescue Jesus and prevent him from being torn apart by his friends. The feud continued even after Jesus had been deposited in the manger. The care offered by one never satisfied the other. What one did, the other redid.

For the congregation it became an unexpected parable of our world, and in the eyes of many, of the church as well. To the outsider, the church often seems composed of many competing factions, all of whom may be sincere, but who seem to divide and destroy the unity Christ came to offer. How can the church be one when so many denominations exist? What role do Presbyterians have or should they play in the one church of Jesus Christ? Why didn't all the Presbyterians join with the Methodists and Congregationalists in forming the United Church in 1925?

The richness and dilemma of being Presbyterian

American Presbyterian Alexander Miller once described himself as "a High Church Presbyterian Reformed Protestant Catholic." That statement, in one phrase, describes both the richness and the dilemma of being a Presbyterian in the world today: richness in that Presbyterians have always seen themselves as an integral part of the one, holy, and catholic church; but a dilemma in that finding a unique role and position among the denominations in Canada today remains a challenge.

Seventy years ago about one-third of the Presbyterians of the day refused to enter the union that brought into being the United Church of Canada. Since then, Presbyterians have suffered from bad press when it comes to ecumenical relations.

In September 1993, John Shelby Spong, a bishop of the Episcopal Church in the United States, visited Vancouver. He issued an enthusiastic endorsement of the United Church and characterized those who did not enter the union of 1925 as "splinter continuing bodies who...represent in every instance the very conservative wing of their traditions."

Bishop Spong grew up as a Presbyterian in a fundamentalist environment in the southern United States. He may have spoken more out of that experience than out of knowledge of the Canadian situation. In any case the historical facts of the situation tell a different story.

Tony Plomp, a Presbyterian minister from Richmond, B.C., replied to Spong in the *Vancouver Sun*:

> The Presbyterian Church, to which Bishop Spong refers, is a body of some 160,000 members who are generally in the middle of the theological spectrum. Since 1925 it has been in the forefront of ecumenical endeavors both on the national and international scene.
>
> It is ironic that Bishop Spong did not realize that our denomination uses the Vancouver School of Theology—hardly a hotbed of conservatism—for the training of its ministers....

Many members and ministers in Presbyterian congregations today have come into the Presbyterian Church from other denominations. I did myself. They may wonder why, in 1925, when the United Church was formed of Congregationalists, Methodists, and Presbyterians, just over 60 percent of the Presbyterians went into the Union while the remainder stayed out.

To be frank, people took these actions for both good and bad reasons. The higher motivations for refusing to join the Union were based on the traditional Presbyterian concern for strong and clear expressions of the historic faith. Opponents rejected the idea that getting together on any basis was more important than truth. It was not sufficient to get together to share feelings and activity, although that too was important. But Presbyterian concern for the intellectual content of the faith expressed in creeds and confessions took precedence over these things.

After Church Union, John McNab, a former editor of the *Presbyterian Record*, recalled that his introduction to Canadian Church Union debate began on an Atlantic liner when he first embarked for Canada. "The speaker was Dr. James Woodsworth, then superintendent of Methodist missions in Western Canada. 'The doctrinal basis of union,' said Woodsworth, 'is a most remarkable document. The articles of its creed are so stated that the Calvinist claims they are Calvinistic and the disciples of Arminius claim them to be Arminian.'"

Arminius lived in the 16th century. The chief emphasis of his theology was on people's freedom, over against Calvin's emphasis on the priority of God's will. This statement of Woodsworth was not good enough for John McNab, nor for the thousands of Presbyterians who refused to enter Union.

Ephraim Scott was editor of the *Presbyterian Record* during the Church Union controversy. Historian Brian Fraser has reconstructed a possible interview with Scott based on Scott's speeches and writings.

To the question of why he resisted Church Union with such vehemence, Scott says the following:

> Interestingly enough, many of us began with a considerable degree of sympathy for the idea of a greater expression of unity among Canada's churches. The idea had been widely discussed in the late 19th century and gained the endorsation of prominent Presbyterians such as Principal William Caven of Knox College and Principal George Munro Grant of Queen's University. But it became increasingly clear, as the plan for organic union took shape between 1904 and 1910, that too much Presbyterianism would be sacrificed in the proposed United Church. The principles upon which we took our stand were truth and freedom. The former was embodied in our system of doctrine, set forth in the Westminster Standards to which our office bearers were bound in their vows of ordination... The principle of freedom found expression in the polity of Presbyterianism. We have a system of church government that allows for the greatest possible freedom within the fellowship of the church and that insists on the independence of the church from any interference from the civil authorities. In the interests of truth and freedom, then, we had to resist the Union movement.

Often, however, Church Union was not opposed on such high principles. Frequently the decisions on the local level revolved around animosities within the congregation, the popularity or lack of such for the local minister and which side he had chosen. Sometimes considerations of property became preeminent. And some even opposed the union on the very un-Presbyterian position that there is only one true church—the Presbyterian Church. Joseph McLelland adapted the words of Mr. Thwackum, Tom Jones's tutor, to assert that, "by religion I mean Christianity, by that I mean Protestantism, and by that Presbyterianism, in fact the continuing Presbyterians in Canada, all 144,000 of them."

But Presbyterians are not against church unions on principle. In recent years, as various unions were consummated in partner churches with whom we work, the General Assembly made it clear that our missionary personnel could enter any local union and, upon returning to Canada, not have their position in our church affected in any way.

Presbyterians agree fully with Ignatius who declared, "Wherever Jesus Christ is, there is the catholic church." The use of the word catholic here means "all-embracing," "world-wide," or "universal." The reformer we most look to, John Calvin, once said that he would gladly cross a thousand seas if it would restore the unity of the church.

The *Westminster Confession of Faith* speaks clearly on this point:

> The catholic or universal Church, which is invisible, consists of the whole number of the elect, that have been, are, or shall be gathered into one, under Christ the head thereof... The visible Church, which is also catholic or universal under the gospel (not confined to one nation, as before under the law), consists of all those throughout the world that profess the true religion, together with their children, and is the Kingdom of our Lord Jesus Christ, the house and family of God...." (25:1–2)

When the *Confession* refers to the "true religion," it means the Christian faith.

So it should not be surprising that a Presbyterian first suggested the talks that eventually led to the United Church of Canada. Some of those who did not enter into the Union hoped to the very end that some kind of federation might be worked out in which all Presbyterians could be involved.

Walter Bryden, an opponent of Church Union in 1925, who later became principal of Knox College, said there was only one reason to either support or oppose Church Union—for the sake of the gospel itself. He stood against Church Union because he saw it primarily as a desire to establish a larger, more efficient, and better organized church in Canada. For him, external organization did not provide a sufficient reason for Church Union.

Presbyterians operate on the premise that there is only one church which God has created. Variety and diversity in that one church are good and in fact enrich the church and strengthen it for its mission. No one part (i.e. denomination) embodies all that God intends the church to be.

Presbyterian life reflects an ecumenical spirit

In that context, the facts of Presbyterian life reflect a deeply-held theological commitment to ecumenism. In times of uncertainty or difficulty, denominations, like people, sometimes tend to withdraw into themselves. Sometimes voices within the Presbyterian Church are heard calling for the denomination to withdraw from such bodies as the World Council of Churches. But those voices do not represent the Presbyterian way. To be Presbyterian means, necessarily, to be involved with other Christians whom we recognize as brothers and sisters in Christ. It means playing our full role in the one, holy, catholic church.

You can see this belief reflected in our current practice and life. For many years Presbyterians have practiced open communion. Christians of whatever denomination are invited to share in the sacrament with us. In 1948, the Canadian Council of Churches reported that Presbyterian donations to European relief were equal to the combined contributions of all other Canadian churches. And from the very formation of The Presbyterian Church in Canada in 1875, we have recognized the baptism and confirmation rites of all other Christian denominations. In our orders of service for these celebrations, the Presbyterian Church is not mentioned; always it is the Church of God, the Church of Jesus Christ, or the Holy Catholic Church.

The Presbyterian Church became a charter member of the Canadian Council of Churches when it was formed in 1944. And in 1948, the Presbyterian Church, along with 147 other churches from 44 countries, joined the World Council of Churches when it was formally constituted in Amsterdam. The World Council of Churches promotes cooperation among denominations in study and action, and is dedicated to fostering an ecumenical spirit among its members.

Our commitment to ecumenism can also seen in the number and quality of leaders the Presbyterian Church has given to the ecumenical movement. You may hear some of the following names bandied about in the Presbyterian Church: Heather Johnston and Ted Johnson, with the World Council of Churches; and Eoin MacKay and Wilfred Butcher, leaders with the Canadian Council of Churches. Donald MacDonald represented our church on the World Alliance of Reformed Churches and for a time was the sole Canadian representative on their executive. Younger leaders are now making their presence felt: Patti Talbot, who worked with the Ecumenical Forum and who is now with the mission department of the United Church; Dawn Ross and Freda Rajotte, who are with the World Council of Churches; and Douglas DuCharme, who served with the Middle East Council of Churches and who is now with the Canadian Council of Churches.

Presbyterians have also been represented and have played an active role in the many church coalitions which have arisen in Canada since the Second World War.

This doesn't mean, of course, that you will never find opponents to the ecumenical movement in the Presbyterian Church. Some of this opposition, now rapidly disappearing, can be traced to bitterness left over from 1925. In the struggle to survive, some Presbyterians became fearful and wished to withdraw from contact with other denominations. Others feared that cooperation with so-called liberal churches might undermine the theological standards and doctrinal purity of our church.

One of those points of controversy occurred in 1947. By that time contact had been reestablished with the Christian Church in China. The Presbyterian Church had already sent missionaries and were in the process of sending more. Some Presbyterians wondered if we should be involved with Christians in this Communist nation. Alex MacDonald, in Heritage Resources, describes how it all came to a head at the General Assembly in 1947.

The Presbytery of Quebec had discussed the subject and

concluded that The Presbyterian Church in Canada should not get involved with the Church of Christ in China. Since 1925, they argued, the Presbyterian Church had affirmed its old name and faith, and to set up these new liaisons only served to waste the church's money and energy and to upset a lot of people. The Presbytery of Quebec sent an overture to the General Assembly saying that the Presbyterian Church should cut off all connections with churches and groups which were not Presbyterian. An overture from the neighboring Presbytery of Montreal came to the same Assembly saying that the best traditions of our church require cooperation with other Christian bodies.

When it came time for the debate, Frank Scott Mackenzie took the floor. In a long but never boring speech, he called on the commissioners to be true to their own traditions. Despite what happened in 1925, he argued, Presbyterians still believed in one church and in working with other Christians.

When he finished, others spoke. When the vote was taken, the General Assembly overwhelmingly agreed to continue their cooperation and partnership with other churches, including the Church of Christ in China.

Ecumenism today and tomorrow

A few years ago I served on a panel at Knox College. The subject for discussion was the church today and where it is headed. Theological students always enjoy ruminating on such subjects. I lamented the fact that Christians were becoming more congregationalistic and individualistic. Their interest centered more on themselves than on the world, or other Christians.

Some of my happiest moments have been with Christians of other denominations. Thirty years ago, in my first parish, we had a close working relationship with all of the other denominations in the town. Unfortunately, that interest and commitment to be involved together has waned. If you have ever tried to help a congregation find a new minister, as I have, you will know that only one thing ranks lower on their list of priorities than denominational concerns, and that is ecumenical relations. I personally feel sad that is the case.

To be true to our traditions and convictions, Presbyterians must be involved in ecumenical councils and coalitions. We do so to bear witness to the oneness of the church, of which all who believe in Jesus Christ are members. And we do so to bring a particular Reformed perspective to the great issues of our time. At times we may not agree with what the World Council or the Canadian Council of Churches says and does. When the World Council gave financial assistance to revolutionary groups in South Africa, many Presbyterians thought this was a mistake and spoke out against it. But we did not withdraw our membership from that organization.

When we disagree, we can become the loyal opposition. But withdrawal from such organizations is counter-productive and disloyal to our tradition. We believe in "one holy catholic apostolic church." To fail to cooperate to the fullest in mission and service with any branch of that church would be to deny our Presbyterian heritage.

In my first pastoral charge, the local association of ministers did not include the Roman Catholic priest largely due to the objections of the pastor of the Church of God. One day, after I had gained his confidence, I said to him, "You know, we really should include the Roman Catholic priest in this association." When he began to list his objections, I countered by saying that, from my viewpoint, he had far more in common with the priest than I had with either of them. If I could welcome the priest into our organization, surely he could.

"Okay," he said, "let's try it."

We did, and as a result, all our lives were enriched and many successful ecumenical services and projects were carried out together.

Christians of other denominations are blood brothers and sisters. As Presbyterians, we have a responsibility to get to know them better so we can work more effectively as part of God's one family.

Chapter 6

Meet your family...

Photo: Canada's Sports Hall of Fame

...as they make the news

Rev. Dr. James Naismith invented basketball in 1891.

Photo: CTV News

...and spread the news

Lloyd Robertson, chief anchor and senior news editor, CTV News.

Several summers ago a friend of mine went to Vancouver to bury his father. Two Presbyterian ministers on holiday on the West coast saw the death in the newspaper and attended my friend's father's funeral. It moved him that they would take time from their holiday to be with him at his father's funeral.

In 1989 our church adopted a Vision Statement which proclaimed: "We will be a loving, inclusive community—truly God's family." All churches strive to become this. But at this point in our history, because we are relatively small it is easier for us to have a real sense that we are indeed a family. Unlike magazines of larger denominations, each month the *Presbyterian Record* carries several pages of pictures of events in local congregations. Most Presbyterians will recognize some of the people in the pictures.

In the following pages we would like to introduce you to some of the members of your Presbyterian and Reformed family, past and present. Some you may know, others you will not. At the end of this section you will find a frame for one of the most important members of this family—YOU.

... at historic moments in history

Photo: Presbyterian Church in Canada Archives

In 1875, four large groups of Presbyterians united to form The Presbyterian Church in Canada. Dr. John Cook was elected Moderator of the first General Assembly, which met in Montreal.

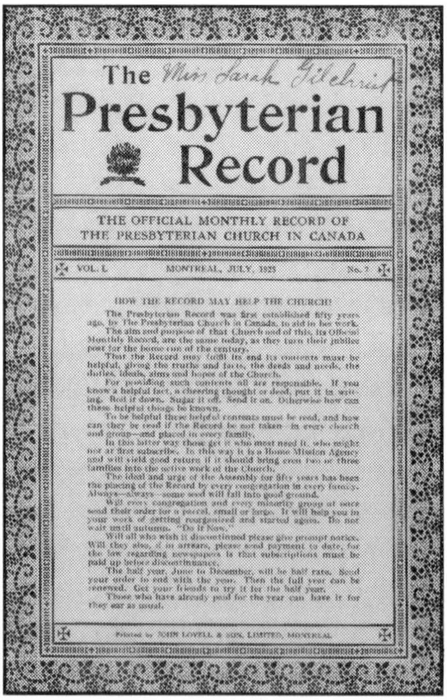

The Miss Sarah Gilchrist

Presbyterian Record

THE OFFICIAL MONTHLY RECORD OF THE PRESBYTERIAN CHURCH IN CANADA

VOL. L — MONTREAL, JULY, 1925 — No. 7

HOW THE RECORD MAY HELP THE CHURCH!

The Presbyterian Record was first established fifty years ago, by The Presbyterian Church in Canada, to aid in her work.

The aim and purpose of that Church and of this, its Official Monthly Record, are the same today, as they turn their jubilee post for the home run of the century.

That the Record may fulfil its end its contents must be helpful, giving the truths and facts, the deeds and needs, the duties, ideals, aims and hopes of the Church.

For providing such contents all are responsible. If you know a helpful fact, a cheering thought or deed, put it in writing. Boil it down. Sugar it off. Send it on. Otherwise how can these helpful things be known.

To be helpful these helpful contents must be read, and how can they be read if the Record be not taken in every church and group—and placed in every family.

In this latter way those get it who most need it, who might not at first subscribe. In this way it is a Home Mission Agency and will yield good return if it should bring even two or three families into the active work of the Church.

The ideal and urge of the Assembly for fifty years has been the placing of the Record by every congregation in every family. Always—always—some seed will fall into good ground.

Will every congregation and every minority group at once send their order for a parcel, small or large. It will help you in your work of getting reorganized and started again. Do not wait until autumn. "Do It Now."

Will all who wish it discontinued please give prompt notice. Will they also, if in arrears, please send payment to date, for the law regarding newspapers is that subscriptions must be paid up before discontinuance.

The half year, June to December, will be half rate. Send your order to end with the year. Then the full year can be renewed. Get your friends to try it for the half year.

Those who have already paid for the year can have it for [illegible] as usual.

Printed by JOHN LOVELL & SON, LIMITED, MONTREAL

Photo: *Presbyterian Record*

In 1925, about 35 percent of Presbyterians voted against entering the new United Church of Canada. They continued to call themselves The Presbyterian Church in Canada. Dr. Ephraim Scott, editor of the *Presbyterian Record*, was elected Moderator of the General Assemby by those who remained Presbyterian.

...as they witness on the front lines

Right:
Elizabeth Hope Mitchell (L) and Helen Bone (R), were nurses and the first women to serve the church during the Klondike Gold Rush, in Atlin, BC, in 1899.

Photos:
Presbyterian Record

Above: Agnes Hislop (R) and Agnes Conkey (L) with the Red Deer Presbytery van. Summer, 1950.

Right: Rev. Robert Baker, Canadian Armed Forces chaplain.

...as they claim their role

Photo: *Presbyterian Record*

In 1992, Linda Bell became the first woman Moderator of the General Assembly. Congratulating Linda is her predecessor, John Cameron.

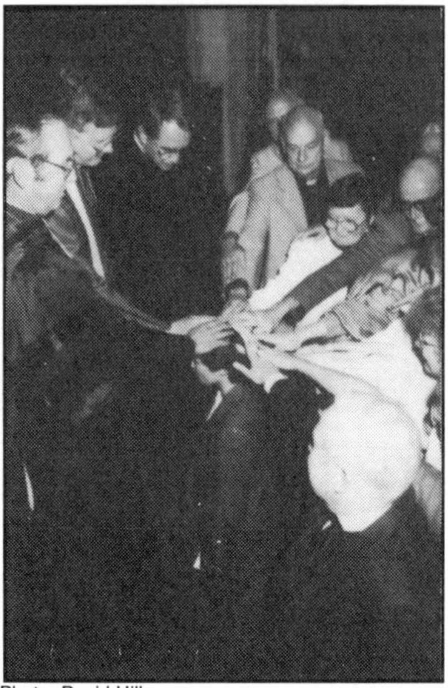

Photo: David Hill

In 1966, after more than ten years of study in committees, congregations, and presbyteries, the General Assembly decided to ordain women as elders and ministers.

Photo: *Presbyterian Record*

Mary Guibault (R), former student at a Presbyterian residential school (Birtle) and now an elder among her people, and her daughter (L) Myra Laramee.

...in the fight for justice

Photo: *Presbyterian Record*

Left: Dr. Akanu Alu Otu,
former Moderator,
The Presbyterian Church of Nigeria.

Photo: Michael Tai

Above: Dr. C.M. Kao
and his wife, Ruth,
three days after his release
from prison in Taiwan.
Dr. Kao had refused to give
information about people
who organized a
demonstration for human
rights.

Photo: *Presbyterian Record*

Left: Vera Chirwa, fights for
human rights in Malawi.

...from around the world

Right: Orphan in Costa Rica being fed by PCC.

Below: Mayan family at worship in Guatemala.

Bottom right: Okokon Udo, pastor in Nigeria.

Bottom left: Debuty Bishop Attila Veres-Kovas and wife, in Romania.

Photo: Wilma Welsh

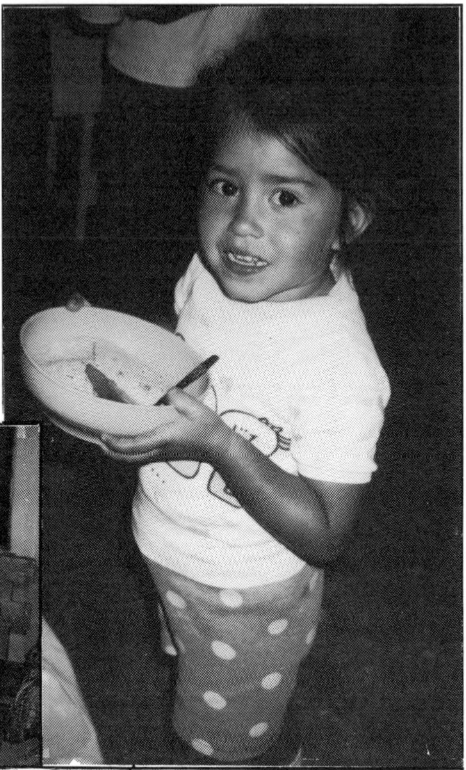

Photo: Wilma Welsh

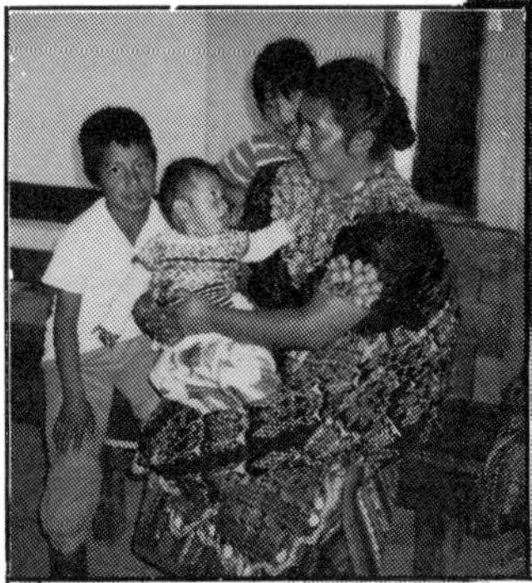

Photo: *Presbyterian Record*

Photo: *Presbyterian Record*

...and as they live their faith here at home.

Photo: *Presbyterian Record*

Above: Rachael Kennedy and Tim Locke, youth observers at the 1993 General Assembly.

Below: David Rankine of Aurora, Ontario, has revived the ancient art form of Celtic illumination.

Photo: *Presbyterian Record*

Photo: *Presbyterian Record*

Above: June Stevenson, editor of *Glad Tidings*.

Why not
put yourself
into the picture?

Chapter 7

Photo: Jim Taylor

The Bible: the book the family lives by

> The Bible is not a collection of answers God has given to our questions: on the contrary, it is the place where God addresses us, where [God] asks *us* the questions *we* have to answer.
> —Jacques Ellul (Reformed Church in France)

I graduated from seminary in 1962 and was preparing to leave for my mission appointment in Saskatchewan when I received a phone call. It came from two elderly ladies who lived in a nearby town. They said they had never met me but had heard about me and wanted to offer me a gift before I began my ministry. I promised to visit them before I left.

And so on the evening before I departed I traveled the 20 kilometers to the home of Jessie and Annie MacKay. The MacKays had been staunch Presbyterians all their lives. Now 89 and 93 years old, they were unable to get out to worship, although they still maintained their own home. They asked that I listen to the story of the Bible they were about to give me.

When they were young children, the newly-arrived Presbyterian minister stayed at their home. Jessie described him as "a Bible pounder." Soon the pulpit Bible in the small country church they attended was falling apart. Their father went off to town to order a new one. Before it arrived, their mother had gathered up the pieces of the old one and sewn it securely together. As a result, the new Bible became a kind of family Bible and was never used as a pulpit Bible.

That Bible, they explained, now resided wrapped in a pillow case in the bottom of a trunk in the corner of their unfinished attic. They would be pleased, they said, if I would now retrieve it so that they might give it to me. I departed with a huge pulpit Bible, now approaching 100 years old, under my arm. Behind me I left two elderly ladies confident they had given me the one thing needful to ensure an effective ministry in the Presbyterian Church.

"People of the book"

This belief, which is frequently referred to as "reverence for the word," is deeply embedded in Presbyterian tradition. A statue of some of the leaders of the Reformation stands in the square in Geneva, Switzerland. John Calvin is portrayed with his hands on the Bible. For Calvin, the Bible alone remained the authoritative source of all religious authority and truth. Little wonder, then, that Presbyterians, along with Jews and Muslims, are often referred to as "people of the book."

In the church I attend, and in many Presbyterian congregations, just before worship begins, someone will come down the aisle carrying the Bible. They will place it on the pulpit or lectern, and then open it. Sometimes this procedure will take place in reverse at the end of the service; the Bible will be closed and carried out of the sanctuary.

At a gathering of some of the members of the congregation where I attend, I enquired if they knew why this was done. I suspected they might answer that it was a convenient way to get the pulpit Bible in and out of the sanctuary. Instead, they delighted me by offering significant theological reasons for this practice.

The actual practice began back in the Middle Ages when Bibles were scarce and were either chained to the pulpit or brought in just before worship and taken out afterward so they wouldn't be stolen.

But today, the carrying in of the Bible signifies to the congregation that worship is about to begin. Opening the Bible tells the worshipers that during this period they can expect to hear God's word both read and expounded from the Bible. The congregation expects to hear, not the personal opinions of the minister, nor a commentary on the news, but a sermon which will illuminate the words and meaning of the Bible.

That does not mean that what is said will not have any meaning for or application to the lives of the listeners. I remember preaching a sermon on Christian stewardship. I talked about the biblical witness which says that all we have is loaned to us from God. We are accountable to God for how we use our talents and gifts, as well as our possessions. I then asked the congregation whether or not, in light of the Bible's teaching, it was good stewardship on our part to use only 12 percent of the property we owned, given the needs we saw around us. The congregation heard this message as a word from God to them. They began to study the needs of their community. Then they made plans. In the end, they tore down most of their facilities and built new ones, which included housing for single-parent families as well as for people with severe disabilities.

The Reformed theologian Karl Barth said that we must always seek to discern God's will with the Bible in one hand and the daily newspaper in the other. Carrying the Bible in at the beginning of worship, however, signifies to all who have gathered that the Bible will play a central role in what happens.

The *Westminster Confession of Faith* begins with a chapter on the Bible. I might wish that it started with a chapter on God, thus being truer to the Reformed faith, but it does illustrate the seriousness with which Presbyterians have always taken the Bible. Indeed, some have suggested that the Bible is the Presbyterian Pope.

This identification of Presbyterians with the Bible began back at the time of the Reformation. Over the years, with varying degrees of consistency and enthusiasm, Presbyterians have submitted all topics of faith and ethics to the question, "What does the Bible say about this?"

At the time of the Reformation, what the church said and what the Bible said came into conflict. In such instances, John Calvin opted in favor of the Bible. Primarily, he said, we must listen for the voice of God in scripture. What the church says and has said is not unimportant, but what the Holy Spirit speaking through the Bible says must always take precedence. The "inward witness of the Holy Spirit," Calvin said, authenticates the Bible's authority for us. God's spirit gives the Bible power to speak to us.

In worship, Calvin would always offer a prayer of illumination before the reading of scripture. This prayer asked God to make the words of the Bible come alive so that people would hear and read them as participants, not spectators.

Calvin saw the potential good of such teaching, but also its pitfalls. The right of people to read scripture for themselves and to be influenced to action by the work of the spirit does not mean that, in terms of biblical interpretation, it's every person for him or herself. Presbyterians with such a philosophy have been responsible for producing more new groups than most denominations.

Stephen Leacock poked fun at Presbyterians for their tendency to divide over minor points of doctrine in his tale entitled "The Rival Churches of St. Asaph and St. Osoph." St. Osoph, he tells the reader, was so Presbyterian it refused to be connected with any other church:

> It seceded some forty years ago...and later on, with three other churches, it seceded from the group of seceding congregations. Still later it fell into a difference with three other churches on the question of eternal punishment, the word 'eternal' not appearing to the elders of St. Osoph's to designate a sufficiently long period. (*Arcadian Adventures with the Idle Rich*, McClelland & Stewart, 1959.)

Perry F. Rockwood, who for years broadcasted *The People's Gospel Hour* from the Maritimes, graduated from Knox College in 1943. He left the denomination because he did not feel Presbyterians were evangelical enough. I once served as minister of Knox Church in Hamilton, Ontario. One of my predecessors in the last quarter of the 19th century was A.B. Simpson. Simpson became convinced the Presbyterian Church was not missionary enough. As a result, he left the Presbyterians and founded a new denomination: the Christian Missionary and Alliance Church.

Recognizing the potential for splitting when members are urged to study the Bible for themselves under the guidance of the Holy Spirit, Presbyterians encourage their members to study the Bible in groups. This form of Bible study encourages members to listen to each other and to take into consideration what the church has taught historically.

Of equal importance was Calvin's principle that scripture must be interpreted by scripture. "The infallible rule of interpretation of Scripture is the Scripture itself," says the *Westminster Confession*. This principle prevents a person from taking some isolated text and applying it in a literalistic fashion detached from the rest of the Bible.

For example, in Romans 13 Paul talks about the Christian's obligation to secular authority. Overall, Paul had great admiration for Roman law, and well he should have. As a Roman citizen himself, it provided pretty good personal security—a whole lot better than Blue Cross! The peace Rome had secured in the empire made it possible for Paul to travel widely and freely. If the Mediterranean had been balkanized, as it has been ever since, Christianity might not have gotten out of the Middle East.

By the time the book of Revelation had been written, though, Christians were about as popular as Jews in Nazi Germany. No longer could the Christian serve the state and Christ. It was one or the other. The writer of Revelation had little good to say about the ruling powers and saw disobedience to their authority as equivalent to obeying God.

These examples show why it is absolutely critical that the Bible be read in its historical context. One can not simply read the meaning from the text without a serious consideration of why, and where, and over against what the original text was written.

Despite the danger of individualistic interpretations, Calvin believed it to be essential to get the Bible back into people's hands. The fact that the Bible is carried in at the beginning of the service by a layperson, never the clergy, also symbolizes this emphasis of Presbyterianism. The people are to know and use the laws, the prophets, and the gospels.

When John Knox left Calvin in Geneva and returned to Scotland to lead the Reformation there, he carried this conviction with him. He immediately began to encourage the translation of the Bible into the language of the people. He set up small study groups in which people could hear and study the Bible. Knox was confident that, by this means, the Holy Spirit would speak through the Bible to direct the church, that Christians would experience a new sense of freedom, and that spiritual revival would sweep the nation. He was not disappointed.

The authority of the Bible today

But what about today? Can we have the same faith that the Bible can help us to decipher the difficult questions we face and provide spiritual sustenance for our lives? Behind many of the tough issues which face the church today lies the question of the authority of the Bible. Christians today are divided over what role the Bible should have in their lives.

Presbyterians stand between two extreme positions. On the one hand, there are those who view the Bible like any other important book. In deciding the great moral and ethical dilemmas of the day, they put the Bible alongside other authorities such as tradition and their own personal experience. When making a decision, they give each of these equal weight.

At the other end of the spectrum are those who believe in verbal inspiration. They hold that each word in the Bible was literally inspired and dictated by God, word-for-word, and therefore should be followed in a literal way. But even people who take this position do not necessarily follow all of the cultic rules and laws prescribed in Leviticus. For example, stoning every adulterer to death, as Leviticus mandates, might solve the problem of over-population, but few Christians today would be prepared to accept, let alone apply, such a law. Even the literalists, then, admit that some parts of the Bible were intended for a particular time and place in history.

Wayne Allen, writing in the May 1994 *Presbyterian Record*, comments on the tendency of those who take the Bible literally to be selective in their use of biblical passages. In other words, they tend to ignore certain passages, or at least give them a secondary role when it comes to authority.

Commenting on some of the laws found in Leviticus, he indulges in comic exaggeration to make his point:

> Leviticus 18:22 contains a list of prohibitions and rules, including some involving leprosy. Leprosy, back then, meant "loathsome skin disease" and included psoriasis, eczema and, probably, bad dandruff. My mother used to attend my congregation until I read Leviticus. She has psoriasis, so I've sent her to the town dump. I also pitched the pork, lobster, oysters, clams, and mussels, for good measure.

Presbyterians here, as in so many places, take a middle ground. For them the Bible holds a unique authority in their lives. But they do not claim the Bible is an authority in all areas of life. That would be to claim more for the Bible than it claims for itself.

The stated purpose of a church-school lesson I once saw said: "To show Moses used many advanced scientific techniques." So what if you could actually demonstrate the thesis, what would you have proven? That Moses was a very clever person? Paul claims God uses the weak to shame the wise. That God reveals scientific secrets to followers which he does not share with others? Such a theory flies in the face of Jesus' claim that God allows the rain to fall on the just and the unjust. To me, such a lesson holds no significance for Christian faith.

If you wish to know about botany, geology, or astronomy, you should seek guidance from a scientist, not the Bible. But if you wish to encounter and hear God speaking to you, then turn to the Bible. "The Scriptures principally teach," says the answer to the third question of the catechism, using the language of the day, "what man is to believe concerning God, and what duty God requires of man." Presbyterians believe that the Bible sets forth the true meaning and purpose of life. Even more importantly, here alone we discover God's love in Jesus Christ.

In his book *Wishful Thinking*, Frederick Buechner, Presbyterian minister and novelist, says the Bible is about people who, at the same time, can be "both believing and unbelieving, innocent and guilty, crusaders and crooks, full of hope and full of despair."

It is also a book about God, he says.

But, he adds, we find something else in it as well. To help

make his point, he calls on theologian Karl Barth, who said that reading the Bible is like looking out a window and seeing everyone shading their eyes, speaking strange words, and pointing excitedly to the sky. "To read the Bible," says Buechner, "is to try to read the expression on their faces. To listen to the words of the Bible is to try to catch the sound of the queer, dangerous, and compelling words they seem to hear."

When I was ordained I was asked the question: "Do you believe the scriptures are the supreme standard in matters of faith and life?" I answered, "yes," and went on to say that, when I became involved with the Bible, God came alive for me. Through the Bible I encountered Jesus Christ, and experienced new life and direction for my life. "The Bible," said Martin Luther, "is the cradle in which Christ is laid."

Hearing the word of God in the Bible is something like listening to Bing Crosby on an old 78 R.P.M. record. We hear Bing, but we also hear other noises—sounds made in the manufacture of the record, and scratches that have accumulated over the years. We must listen attentively in order to distinguish between the two.

Presbyterians approach the Bible with a good deal of respect. Not as a kind of Presbyterian crucifix or good luck charm, but out of the conviction that Jesus Christ will become a living, guiding presence for us in its pages. When that happens, the Bible becomes, as the writer of Hebrews puts it, "...living and active, sharper than any two-edged sword...discerning the thoughts and intentions of the heart." (Hebrews 4:12)

I sometimes suspect that very sophisticated interpretations of the Bible hide an unwillingness to have our lives guided by it. It's not so much that we don't understand the Bible as that we understand it, but don't like its message.

Because we take the Bible so seriously, among Presbyterians you should discover people who treat the Bible with more respect than any other Christians. In Presbyterian churches, you should find more Bible studies. Presbyterian ministers should be more highly skilled and trained in biblical interpretation than any other clergy. Unfortunately this is not always the case.

However, often when Christians of all stripes gather to discuss the great issues of our time, Presbyterians are expected to contribute a learned and careful exposition of the relevant scriptures. In many theological seminaries of other denominations, students no longer have to study the original languages in which the Bible was written (Hebrew in the case of the Old Testament, Greek for the New Testament). When I attended seminary in the 1960s, I had to learn both Greek and Hebrew. Even today, knowledge of at least one of the biblical languages is required for ordination by our church.

Young people today may find it hard to believe that in the young people's group I attended as a teenager we engaged in heated debates about such deep theological issues as predestination and God's providence, particularly in terms of what the Bible taught on those subjects.

Engaged by the Bible

As a Presbyterian it is important to be engaged daily by the Bible. Some like to use a devotional guide for this purpose. Many such guides are available. The one our denomination contributes to and helps to produce is called *These Days*. For each day of the week a scripture passage, commentary, and brief prayer is provided.

Many people have found the series of daily Bible readings of Scottish theologian William Barclay helpful.

The Bible Society provides a list of readings which enables you to read the whole Bible in three years.

Recently, the Presbyterian Church (U.S.A.) produced the *Book of Common Worship: Daily Prayer*. A feature of this book I particularly like is a daily lectionary with readings which follow the Church Year. It is based on a two-year cycle. If followed, after two years, a person will have read the New Testament twice and the Old Testament once.

Other people like to follow their own pattern, perhaps reading a chapter a day from both the Old and New Testaments.

But whatever you do, you will need a good modern translation of the Bible. Personally, I like the *New Revised Standard Version* plus a good commentary to help me over the difficult places.

While I served in my last congregation, a new study on the Bible, called Kerygma, was introduced. Since then, many congregations and denominations have used it. Although this study was rigorous and demanding, for those willing to put forth the effort it was also tremendously rewarding. Some excellent lay leaders in our congregation willingly gave their time, so that, at one point, we had almost 100 people participating in this study. While it was going on, I could not help feeling that not only were we engaging in something all Christians needed to do at this time in our history, but we were being most true to our own roots and history.

We do not always take the Bible with such seriousness. Failure to do so, however, means we fail to respond to the heartbeat of our own tradition.

Chapter 8

Photo: *Presbyterian Record*

St. Mark's Presbyterian Church, North York, Ontario.

Worship: family get-togethers

The fathers of the Reformed Churches sought to make the people actual participants in public worship, instead of mere spectators or listeners.

—Sandford Fleming

When I was growing up, next to Christmas, I enjoyed Lent the best—but for wrong, sadistic reasons. I really had no idea what Lent was about. For me it was simply get-even time with the Roman Catholics.

For the rest of the year, or so it seemed to me, Protestants, and particularly Presbyterians, got the dirty end of the stick. We attended church at least once, and sometimes twice, on Sundays, as well as Sunday school in the afternoons. The Presbyterian tradition of keeping the "Sabbath day holy" still lived—no ball games or fun the rest of the day.

But my Roman Catholic friends lived in a different world. They went to mass and did pretty much what they wanted the rest of the day, or so it seemed to me.

But all that changed during Lent. Roman Catholics were suddenly struck by a whole bunch of oppressive regulations from which I was totally free. They went to mass early in the morning while I slept in. They gave up things, the best things in life for a young boy, such as gum, and chocolate bars, and dancing.

Today all of that has changed. Christians of whatever stripe learn from each other. The celebration of Lent now enriches the lives of Presbyterians. In congregations which I have served, Lent has become the season for additional worship and service, a time for preparing for Holy Week and the celebration of Easter. Presbyterians have learned that Lent can add much to their spiritual lives.

Participating in worship

At the same time, Presbyterians should cherish and practice aspects of their own tradition which carry the potential to meet the needs of people today. One of these is the importance of the worshiper as an actual participant in worship.

John Calvin attempted to recover this notion during the Reformation. During the time prior to the Reformation, the church tended to treat the ordinary worshiper as unimportant to the whole process. Calvin tried to reverse this tendency and designed worship so that the people could feel they were a part of it.

At the beginning of this century, a famous Canadian Presbyterian concerned himself with precisely this question. On August 20, 1898, Sandford Fleming wrote to the convener of the General Assembly's Committee on Worship, Professor James Ross. Fleming, better known as Sir Sandford Fleming, laid out the route for the transcontinental railway. He was also a devout and lifelong Presbyterian. The state of worship in the Presbyterian Church at the turn of the century concerned Fleming.

In his letter to Ross, he admits that he has no special right to address Ross, having held no office in the church. He says, however, that he has "...been a regular attendant at the services of the church since my infancy, about three score and ten years ago, and during those years I have had opportunities of judging the needs of my fellow worshipers under all circumstances, and of the merits and defects of the ordinary services of our congregations."

Fleming's chief concern was the lack of participation by the people in worship. Worship, for Fleming, consisted of two parts. The first involved listening to God speak through the reading of scriptures, and the preaching. This part of worship he was content to leave in the hands of clergy.

Not so the second part of worship—praise and prayer. Praise, he felt, was adequately looked after by a hymnbook through which all participate in God's worship. However, he worried about the prayers which had been reduced to extemporaneous prayer by the minister. Unlike the hymns, in the prayers people no longer even had the opportunity to utter an audible "amen." He argued against leaving all the praying in the hands of the local minister, whom he said may have no gift for extemporaneous prayer, or who may be governed in his prayers from Sunday to Sunday more by the state of his health than his piety.

Fleming had no desire to turn to the practice of some denominations whereby prayers were limited to those prescribed in a book. But he was obviously tired of worshiping under ministers whose prayers were repetitious, disorganized, and largely irrelevant to the worshiper. He laid responsibility for the situation at the feet of the Puritans who, reacting to having an English prayer book forced on them, went too far in banning all written prayers. In fact, the Puritans wanted to give maximum participation to the laity too, but in practice their protest led to more dominance by the clergy.

Fleming asked for a return to the practice of Calvin and Knox, when "all Reformed churches were...liturgical."

"Our people are passive..." he protested.

He asked Ross for a service book, or aids for worship, or "at least a collection of people's prayers, sanctioned by the General Assembly, in each pew." With such prayers, carefully prepared and printed beforehand, he believed, the confession, thanksgivings, and intercessions could be more adequately expressed. Fleming had no desire to do away with extemporaneous prayer altogether. He only asked that there be both kinds of prayer.

By making these calls for reform in worship, Fleming called the church back to the very heart and meaning of the word "worship." Worship derives from the idea of worth. God is worthy of our praise. The Greek word for worship, liturgy, literally means the work of the people. Worship, then, is the praise and honor people pour out before God.

I have a lot of sympathy for Fleming's concerns. In the environment in which I grew up, if the minister read a prayer he was considered insincere. Everyone was expected to keep their eyes closed during the prayers, including the preacher. The pastoral prayer, in particular, was extremely long.

Frequently, in my childhood congregation, a stop on the organ would stick, creating a continuing sound of variable pitch echoing throughout the sanctuary. The organist would wait for the long prayer. He would then proceed to the back of the choir, dislodge a panel in the wall, and disappear. Eventually, the sound would cease, a sign to the minister, I suspected, that he could soon bring his prayer to a conclusion.

Extemporaneous prayers also had a certain predictability about them. Most had a fairly standard list of topics and phrases. The mind easily wandered onto other things.

Thankfully, in most Presbyterian churches today, you will find the mixture Fleming advocated. Some prayers will be offered extemporaneously by the minister, some may be adapted from the *Book of Common Order* (a book of prayers and orders of service approved by the church, for voluntary use), and others may be carefully prepared beforehand by the minister. Often the congregation will join in responsive or unison prayers.

Still, one might wonder whether Fleming's plea for greater participation by the laity in worship has been adequately met by these changes in present worship practice.

The order of worship

Since Fleming wished to get back to the practices of the Reformation, we might ask what worship was like then. Obviously worship was important for Calvin. He had delineated three marks of a true church. Two of them, the right preaching of the word and the right administration of the sacraments, concern worship. The third was discipline.

As in everything else, Calvin believed that worship should

conform to what could be discerned in the Bible and what was practiced by the early church. This meant restoring the spirit and simplicity of worship, which Calvin believed lay at the heart of the early worship of the church. In practice, this meant the service must be in the language of the people. There must be a return to biblical preaching, and there should be frequent celebrations of the Lord's Supper for **all** Christians. In the church before the Reformation, worship was conducted in Latin, a language the ordinary people did not understand. The priests, but not the people, celebrated the mass frequently. And in many places, biblical preaching had just about disappeared.

Wishing to follow the Bible for hymn texts, Calvin allowed only paraphrases of Psalms, and none of the gospel songs so popular with Luther and the Lutherans. Today that has changed. The hymnbook in use today, called the *Book of Praise*, has a great variety of gospel hymns, although it retains a large section of metrical Psalms. Published in 1972, it was a revision of its predecessor from 1918, which itself was a revision of an 1897 book. As I write, in 1995, a new book is being prepared.

The music in many worship services today is supplemented by additional contemporary songbooks, or perhaps a selection put together by the local congregation. Some congregations are taking advantage of licensing programs which offer them the opportunity to copy and use thousands of different religious songs and hymns. Different companies provide this service. The publisher of this book administrates one such program called *LicenSing*.

Calvin's service had two parts: The Liturgy of the Word, and The Liturgy of the Upper Room.

He began the service with the reading of Psalm 124, verse 8: "Our help is in the name of the Lord, who made heaven and earth."

Prayers of confession and pardon followed. "We begin," he wrote in the preface to his service book of 1545, "with confession of our sins, adding verses from the Law and Gospel [words of assurance of pardon and forgiveness]." Having been assured of forgiveness, "...we continue with psalms, hymns of praise, the reading of the Gospel, the confession of faith [Apostles' Creed], and the holy oblations and offerings..."

After a metrical psalm, a prayer for illumination was offered, followed by the reading of scripture and the sermon.

In response to the sermon, alms for the poor were collected and prayers for others offered. "It follows," he wrote, "that we must pray for the salvation of all men, for the life of Christ should be greatly enkindled within us."

The intercessions concluded with the Lord's Prayer, followed by communion if it was celebrated. Calvin sought to celebrate weekly communion, an ideal he never attained. Following reception of the elements, again in Calvin's words, we conclude "the whole Mystery with praise and thanksgiving."

Calvin's order of service, then, would have looked something like this:

THE LITURGY OF THE WORD

Scripture sentence (Psalm 124:8)
Confession of sins
Prayer for pardon
Metrical Psalm
Prayer for understanding
Scripture readings
Sermon

THE LITURGY OF THE UPPER ROOM

Collection of gifts for the poor
Prayers for others
Lord's Prayer
Preparation of bread and wine for communion
Apostles' Creed
Words from the Bible describing first communion
Exhortation
Prayer of consecration for the bread, wine, and the participants
The breaking of the bread
The people receive the bread and wine while a psalm or other scripture is read
Prayers
Blessing

Calvin believed that this order of worship agreed with "the ancient Church of the Apostles, martyrs, and Holy Fathers."

You might wish to compare the service used in your congregation with the one used by Calvin. You will not likely find many differences.

In a recent essay, Stephen Farris, professor at Knox College in Toronto, outlined what he considers to be the main characteristics of Presbyterian worship over the centuries. Preaching of the Word of God will enjoy a central place, he says.

In the church of my childhood, the central, elevated pulpit left no doubt, visually at least, as to the importance of the sermon. Everything in the service seemed to point towards the sermon, and when it ended, so did the service, or nearly—a brief prayer, a closing hymn, and the benediction was all that remained. You will seldom attend a Presbyterian service of worship without hearing a sermon and giving an offering.

Presbyterians have also recognized the danger of the Bible being used by preachers to reinforce their own pet themes. That is why the *Westminster Directory of Public Worship* (produced in the 17th century to give guidance to the church regarding worship) suggested that a kind of lectionary be used. Lectionaries provide a systematic reading of the Bible so that most of the Bible will be covered over a period of time. The *Westminster Directory* advised that at each service a significant portion be read from both the Old and New Testaments, and that the following week preachers should take up where they left off and preach from the passages as they come up.

Today, many Presbyterians follow some kind of lectionary. But again, this use which many have found helpful is always voluntary. At any point a minister may decide to leave the lectionary to present a series of sermons from a particular part of the Bible, or to deal with pressing issues of the day.

Presbyterians recognize two sacraments: baptism, and the Lord's Supper or communion. As Farris points out, Presbyterians view them primarily as God's action, rather than as human responses to God. Through the sacraments, God reaches down to feed and nurture God's people.

Simplicity in worship

Presbyterians attempt to carry out all of this in an atmosphere of simplicity.

I thought about this as I sat in the congregation I now attend and watched a young couple come in and take a seat near the front of the sanctuary. I had not seen them before and they were obviously unfamiliar with how we did things. They frequently looked back over their shoulders to get a clue as to what to do next. The choir, which sometimes can offer guidance in these matters, was of no help in this instance. Members had taken their customary places in the choir gallery at the rear of the sanctuary; liturgically correct, perhaps, but not useful to newcomers looking for help so they won't embarrass themselves.

I wondered if we had made the worship experience too complicated in our desire to be liturgically correct. Had we abandoned the traditional value Presbyterians place on simplicity to the detriment of making newcomers or outsiders feel welcomed and appreciated?

The other day I looked at an order of service which my brother (also a Presbyterian minister) uses. It was so simple I wondered at first why he had put it down on paper. There were prayers and a lesson or two, a sermon (of course), and music—lots of music, much of it contemporary. Missing were most of the things I have become accustomed to: the Apostles' Creed, the *Gloria Patri*, and the various responses of the people—things which, as an insider, I take for granted, but for an outsider or someone new must seem strange and confusing.

I doubt if my brother designed his service to recover a sense of the beauty of Presbyterian simplicity. Instead he did it so that a first-time visitor could participate without the fear of embarrassment which results from doing one thing when everyone else does something else. In the last 15 years, his congregation has been one of the fastest growing in our denomination.

People today, especially young people who may have little familiarity with the traditions of the church, enjoy informality and simplicity in worship. This strength in our tradition should not be abandoned.

Presbyterians oppose an unalterably-fixed order of worship, but, as explained earlier, they are not opposed to prayers from a book. In 1991 a new *Book of Common Worship* was introduced to the church. It will gradually replace the *Book of Common Order* prepared in 1922 and revised in 1964. Like its predecessors, this new book contains prayers for almost every occasion, and suggested orders of service for both regular services and special occasions. Also like its predecessors, when the General Assembly adopted it, it was accepted for voluntary use in the church. In other words, a minister may choose to use it, or not to use it, at his or her own discretion.

This *Book of Common Worship*, loose-leaf and almost 500 pages, at first blush seems pretty wordy. But it contains lots of opportunities to enrich worship. Along with suggestions for familiar services of baptism, marriage, funerals, and of Word and Sacraments, there are services for the blessing of a civil marriage, and the renewal of marriage vows.

The *Book of Common Worship* also contains resources for ministering to the sick, which include prayers, and a service for anointing and the laying on of hands. In this latter type of service, the minister and elders will visit a sick person, physically place their hands on that person, and pour oil over them as they pray. This practice goes back to the New Testament.

The book contains brief ceremonies to welcome a new baby, to celebrate the anniversary of a baptism (something which Presbyterians make too little of), and to offer thanksgiving for a new home. It even includes graces for meals.

Prayers are both modern and traditional. One prayer, in the latter category, caught my attention. I have often heard it used and have always been inspired by it.

"O Lord, support us all the day long, until the shadows lengthen, the evening comes, the busy world is hushed, the fever of life is over, and our work is done. Then, Lord, in your mercy grant us safe lodging, a holy rest, and peace at last; through Jesus Christ our Lord."

What I didn't know is what the *Book of Common Worship* tells me. This prayer was used by John Henry Newman in the 19th century, and probably originated in the 16th century.

At the other end of the scale is this contemporary prayer which caught my eye: "Thanksgiving for a New Pet."

> Gracious God...we give you thanks and praise for our new pet,____________, which has been given into our care. May we find joy in him/her, take good care for him/her, play with

him/her, and love him/her. May we honor you through our care of this your creature. We pray in the name of the One who cared for all, Jesus Christ our Savior.

I know my dog, Tasha, would be pleased with such a prayer and would wish that her family would pray it often. Sandford Fleming would also be happy with such a book, but probably not be content until it appeared in every pew.

Resource books like the *Book of Common Worship* can add depth and feeling to both our public and personal devotions and are very much a part of our Presbyterian tradition.

Connecting worship and the world

Farris also notes that Presbyterian worship has always emphasized the connection between worship and the world.

In a congregation I once served, large plain-glass windows ran to the floor on both sides of the sanctuary. The congregation insisted they remain as clear glass, not because they were too cheap to install stained glass, but to ensure that the world could never be shut out from their worship. Recently, stained glass **was** installed, but only after a compromise had been reached. The stained-glass windows had to be light enough to allow people to still see through them to the world beyond.

Today, within the principles I have outlined, and given the freedom Presbyterians are permitted, you will experience great variety in the way Presbyterians worship.

In Montreal, for example, in the Church of St. Andrew and St. Paul, you will experience what many would describe as the best of a more liturgical form of Presbyterian worship. The Gothic cathedral style of the stone building itself inspires reverence and awe. The sanctuary breathes history, its membership from times past reading like a "Who's Who" of Canadian history—McGill, Redpath, Strathcona, Penfield. Worship here is formal: written prayers are carefully prepared; at communion, male elders wear morning coats and female elders dress in black; and always there is a metrical psalm. But the congregation is not afraid of change. Scripture readings come from a modern translation, the prayers are in contemporary speech, and the sermon, which retains a prominent place, seeks to speak to the contemporary situation. The large choir, many of whom are paid professionals, lead the music which has been drawn from church music originating through the ages.

A sharp contrast to this high, formal Presbyterian worship takes place in the Caribou region of central British Columbia. Here David Webber ministers to a number of house churches. Informality replaces formality, the strum of the guitar replaces the chords of the pipe organ, and a living room replaces the Gothic cathedral.

Or go to the other side of Canada, Prince Edward Island, and the four-point charge of Murray Harbour North. From the pulpit of Peter's Road Church, the minister can look through the Gothic frames of this century-old church, across the orderly fields to the blue sea. In these churches, farmers and fishermen gather Sabbath by Sabbath, just as their covenanting forebears did a century ago when they arrived from Galloway towns such as Lockerbie, Ecclefechan, and Dumfries.

But let their minister, Gael Matheson, describe worship as experienced in these island congregations:

> The Word of God is central to their worship. Borne in with all due reverence by the robed beadle, the congregation rises at its entry. In turn, responsive Psalm, Old Testament Lesson, Epistle, and the Gospel of our Lord Jesus Christ. It is to his Gospel that they turn for their deeper security, consolation, assurance, and resolution of the most extreme polarities. Worship, therefore, is ordered to move towards and from the Word and its sharing: hymns, choruses, anthems, youth talk, prayers and offerings all. The language is largely traditional; "thee" and "thou" and God as Father are quite at home in the hearts of rural Island Presbyterians. The praise is fervent as it is evangelical—by choice; hymns that personalize the gospel as well as witness to that good profession where country shyness and/or Celtic laconicism otherwise may fail them.

On any Sunday in Presbyterian churches across Canada, you will hear people worshiping in a variety of languages, including French, Korean, Hungarian, Italian, Spanish, Portuguese, Ukrainian, Arabic, Taiwanese, Chinese, and languages of the aboriginal peoples. Some of these groups, such as the Koreans, result from immigration from countries which have large Presbyterian populations. Others, like the Italian church in Toronto, are a result of recent efforts to provide a ministry to these people in Canada.

For 11 years I served as a pastor in Toronto. We shared our facilities with a Korean congregation. I remember the first time I preached during a Korean service. The congregation expressed disappointment. The 20-minute sermon was too short; they had expected at least 40 minutes. Despite this difference, Korean Presbyterians worship much like the rest of us. By sitting in services conducted in another language, I learned that there is much more to worship than what my mind can understand and process. Often I wouldn't understand a word, but the body language of the people, the joyful exuberance of their singing, and the expressions on their faces made it clear to me that this was genuine worship. The quiet devotion and prayer of Korean Christians add to our understanding of what it means to worship God with our whole being.

The other day I interviewed a young minister from the church in Nigeria. He had visited a number of our churches in Canada and what he saw concerned him. He noticed that people only became animated during the coffee hour after worship. That same enthusiasm never seemed to enter their worship. He wondered why. "In Nigeria," he said, "we believe in worshiping God with body, mind, and emotion." Next time you attend worship, look around and see what the body language, the way the people sing and participate, tells you about the inportance and value of the worship.

During the past year I have enjoyed an association with a Chinese Presbyterian Church on the edge of Chinatown in Toronto. Each Sunday they provide two services. One is traditional, conducted in the Chinese language. The other, held in the gymnasium of the church, attracts about 400 young people to worship and is led by guitar and piano. Young people are not afraid to share part of their spiritual journey in order to witness to and encourage others. Their young pastor addresses the issues they face each day. For me, it provides a wonderful example of a group who fully exploits the freedom Presbyterians enjoy to worship God in a variety of forms.

In Canada, the debate over whether to allow the use of the organ in worship, known as the organ controversy, was fought out in the Presbyterian Church in the middle of the 19th century. Before that, most Presbyterian congregations allowed no instrumental music except a precentor who used a tuning fork to establish pitch.

As organs began to be introduced, many people objected saying the organ was "the instrument of the devil." This "kist [chest] of whistles," as its detractors derisively called it, would destroy the "purity of worship." But supporters argued that the organ was necessary to attract the youth and to appeal to Canadians of non-Scottish background.

Sir John A. Macdonald's home church in Kingston, Ontario, went modern in 1889 by introducing an organ. When the church burned down shortly afterward, many believed it was because they had installed an organ.

Similar debates about music and instruments still echo through our congregations today. The organ is now firmly established as the instrument of choice in most Presbyterian congregations. From being "an instrument of the devil," the organ has become "the sacred instrument," often used to the exclusion of all other instruments. Today, people in our churches argue that instruments other than the organ must be used. Instruments such as the keyboard, guitar, and drums, which are more attuned to today's culture, attract young people and those no longer drawn by the familiar strains of the organ.

Learning from others

Still you won't find many Presbyterians who play the tambourine—at least not in worship. But within the strictures of dignity and respect for God you will discover a remarkable variety in the forms and ways that Presbyterians worship. Part of this comes from what we have learned and are learning from other branches of Christ's church.

We are learning that God can be worshiped with colors and drama, not only with our minds. Many Presbyterians use, to their benefit, the *Common Lectionary* or the *Revised Common Lectionary* which many of their brothers and sisters in other denominations also use. This practice cannot but aid our common growth in Christ. At the same time, we too have contributions to make to the praise offered up to God throughout the earth. It is not disloyal to learn from others—only to neglect one's own rich tradition.

George MacLeod, founder of the Iona Community in Scotland, responded to the challenge to "get back to the worship of our fathers," by asking, "Which of our fathers?" Presbyterian worship has always evolved and changed. Perhaps the one constant has been our emphasis that worship must never be simply the sharing of personal experiences, but rather the celebration of God's action. George MacLeod was right when he wrote in *Only One Way Left* that, "The true Presbyterian is challenged by the prompting of the Holy Spirit as he speaks to our day."

An optional exercise?

Unfortunately, for some Presbyterians today worship has become an optional exercise. Such would have been unthinkable for most of their forebears.

At the 1992 General Assembly, Brian Fraser, from the Vancouver School of Theology, addressed this question with a story.

When Jock retired, Geordie suddenly and without explanation stopped going to church. Jock didn't say anything for the first couple of weeks, but finally decided to raise the issue when they got together to play cribbage that week. They sat together in Geordie's kitchen on a cold fall night before a glowing coal fire.

In the midst of the rubber match, Jock said, "I haven't seen you in church the last couple of Sundays."

"No, you haven't," responded Geordie.

"Been sick?"

"No."

"Not impressed with the new minister?"

"Not really."

"Think you'll be back soon?"

"I doubt it."

"Well, I must admit that I find that rather disturbing," mused Jock.

"I thought you probably would," said Geordie.

Jock reached for the tongs beside the fireplace, removed a single glowing lump of coal from among the others, and set it by itself on the hearth. They sipped on their drams of whisky and smoked their pipes as they watched it burn out and die. Jock rose, buttoned his coat, and went out into the cold autumn night. The next Sunday, Geordie was back in the sanctuary.

Chapter 9

Rev. Chris Vais baptizes Zachary Fisher.

The sacraments: the family gathers around table and font

> Sacraments are "outward and visible signs of an inward and spiritual grace."
>
> —a common definition of the sacraments

I was the first person in my family to become a full member of the Presbyterian Church. I became a member in my late teens and was baptized as an adult. Having been brought up a Baptist, I had not been "done," as they say in the vernacular. Interestingly, it was the sacraments, specifically baptism, which for many years proved to be the stumbling block which prevented my parents from becoming members of a Presbyterian church. For them, baptism meant "believer's baptism." They could not comprehend how baptism administered to a baby, incapable of understanding, or making decisions, or even knowing what was going on, could have any effect.

In my parents' objections to infant baptism, we see highlighted the most important thing Presbyterians believe about the sacraments. In a sacrament, God acts towards us. We celebrate what God has done and is doing, not our own actions.

The sacraments, Calvin said, are "a testimony of God's favor toward us, confirmed by an outward sign, with a mutual testifying of our godliness toward him."

I like Saint Augustine's definition of a sacrament: "the Word made visible." Or that of Scottish theologian Donald Baillie: "a making present of the living Christ."

The Reformers frequently described sacraments as seals. In their day, when a king made a decree his words were written down and read aloud to the people. But the decree was not official until the king's seal was affixed to it. The seal made it authentic. If hearers could see the seal, they knew the proclamation was not spurious, the king himself was speaking to them.

That's what sacraments do for us; they make real in our persons the good news we hear proclaimed. In the same way, Jesus did not just talk about the kingdom, but provided visible signs of its presence by touching lepers and healing the sick.

Roman Catholics and the Eastern Orthodox recognize seven sacraments. The Salvation Army and Quakers have none. Presbyterians, along with most other Protestants, say there are two sacraments. Only baptism and the Lord's Supper, they argue, are given explicit authorization by Jesus in the Bible.

Quakers make a good point when they argue that since all places, moments, and actions can be holy, no particular ones should be set apart in a way that would deny the holiness possible elsewhere. But the opposite can also be true. The sacraments can be viewed as epitomizing or focusing all of the rest of our lives.

At one time, the Lord's Supper clearly revealed this connection. Bread, actually milled and baked by the participants, and grapes grown and stomped on by their feet to make wine, were brought as symbols of the worshipers' whole life raised and offered to God.

Presbyterians take the sacraments seriously even if they do not fully understand their meaning. People will turn out for baptism or communion when they seldom show up at a regular worship service.

Baptism

I remember early in my ministry trying to impress a young couple with the seriousness of the vows they would take when having their infant baptized. I said that the congregation also was involved as part of the baby's family and would take an active role in the child's upbringing. My exhortations must have sounded more like threats because the baby's grandmother reported to a senior minister in the presbytery that Mr. Congram refused to baptize her grandchild. For her that was an unforgivable sin.

Philip Lee, a minister in St. John, New Brunswick, relates a story about meeting a fellow brought up along the Clyde, in Scotland, and at the time of their meeting, working on frigates in the St. John's dry dock. He told Lee the reason he had not been coming to church was that he was an agnostic. But a few months later he dropped by Lee's office. He informed him that some friends of his had adopted a baby girl and wanted "to have the wee lassie done."

"What's their religion?" Lee asked.

"Same as myself," he replied, "Presbyterian."

For such an exciting and important event you may be surprised to find that the actual service in a Presbyterian church is plain and simple. Usually a few drops of water are sprinkled on the baby's head, a few words are spoken, some prayers are said, and the service is complete. Often the greatest excitement comes when the baby begins to scream and drowns out the minister. Sometimes the minister will carry the infant into the congregation and place the child in the arms of a worshiper, symbolizing the child's welcome into the church.

When a Presbyterian minister refuses to conduct a private baptism it is not because he or she wishes to be mean. It is because infant baptism conveys a powerful message about the congregation as family. Baptism is our initiation or adoption into the church family. The whole congregation becomes the "godparent."

In the past, godparents, often another Christian couple, were designated to assist the parents in raising their child in the Christian faith. This responsibility often carried with it financial and legal responsibilities. Today many of these responsibilities have been assumed by the state. Presbyterians are not against having godparents, but have generally viewed these responsibilities as residing in the congregational family in which the child will be raised.

One way a congregation takes seriously this responsibility is by providing a program of Christian education for all stages of the child's growing years.

Usually, then, during the administration of baptism, the congregation will be asked to stand and answer a question something like this: "Our Lord Jesus Christ ordered us to teach those who are baptized. Do you, the people of the church, promise to tell this new disciple [child] the good news of the gospel, to help him/her know all Christ's commands, and, by your fellowship, to strengthen his/her family ties with the household of God?"

Baptized members will be responsible both for the good name of the Christian family and its welfare in the world. For these many reasons Presbyterians prefer to celebrate baptism in the congregational family. For them, private baptisms make no sense.

Presbyterians recognize all the traditional ways of baptizing (immersion, pouring, and sprinkling) as valid. Each method can convey in a special way some aspect of the meaning of baptism. Pouring or sprinkling the water vividly conveys God's spirit coming into the life of the baptized. I should be quick to point out, however, that Presbyterians do not believe that God's action is tied to the actual moment of baptism, or that a person not baptized is bereft of God's presence.

I remember once asking the children about the meaning of the baptism they had just witnessed. It is the sign of our entrance into the family of God, I declared. A small boy raised his hand. "Does this mean," he inquired "that if I am not baptized I am not a part of God's family?" I suddenly realized what I had done. This small boy had come with his family from Atlanta, Georgia, where he had been brought up as a Baptist. Knowing this allowed me to quickly assure him that, although baptism was important, because he had not yet been baptized did not mean he was outside the family.

Baptism is an important way in which God acts in our lives. But Presbyterians do not believe that children who are not baptized will go to hell. Baptism is not a mechanical or magical device. Neither the water nor the clergy who perform the baptism have supernatural powers. On the other hand, just as parents want the best of physical benefits for their children, so they will not neglect baptism, the sign by which they are affirmed as part of God's family.

As a child growing up in the Baptist tradition, services of adult baptism in which the minister took adults into a large tub of water and actually immersed them were always particularly dramatic and memorable. I remember being particularly impressed by one person who insisted that his wallet be immersed in the water with him, a symbol that he would not withhold anything from the Lord.

The symbolic aspect of immersion derives primarily from sin and crucifixion. In going under the water, one dies to sin and evil just as Jesus died, and one is resurrected as one emerges from the water. The practice of sprinkling or pouring takes as its primary metaphor the pouring out of God's grace, which can never be earned or merited but is freely poured out for us.

The most common form practiced among Presbyterians is sprinkling. The minister takes a small amount of water in his or her hand and sprinkles a few drops onto the head of the one being baptized. Normally this will be accompanied by the repeating of the traditional words used during baptism: "[person's name], I baptize you in the name of the Father and of the Son and of the Holy Spirit."

The church baptizes any child when at least one of the child's parents is a Christian. You will find different views among ministers as to what makes a person a Christian. Some will insist that the parent must be an active member in the congregation where the child is baptized. For others it is enough that their name appears on the role, that somewhere in the past they themselves have confessed their faith. For still others it is enough that the parent believes in Jesus Christ, whether or not they have formally been received by the church. Recently, the church also made provision for grandparents or others who are active in the raising of the child to sponsor children for baptism. This might happen when, for whatever reason, the parents of the child are not available to take the baptismal vows.

Infant baptism is based on the idea of a covenant—that God's promises and love are extended "to you and to your children." Peter makes this clear in Acts 2:39: "For the promise is to you and to your children and to all that are far off, everyone whom the Lord our God calls." (*Inclusive Language Lectionary*)

In return, parents promise to bring their children up in this covenant, teaching them the duties and responsibilities of the Christian faith. The hope and expectation is that when these children are able to think and decide for themselves, they will want to confirm for themselves the faith into which they have been baptized.

I interviewed George Vais just before he became Moderator of the Presbyterian Church in 1994. George was born in Greece and lived there as a child. When he was 15, he immigrated to Canada with his family. I asked him when he had become a Christian. He replied that at no time in his life did he not feel a part of the family of God. His parents were members of the Presbyterian church in Greece (Greek Evangelical Church).

Children of believers are literally members of the church when they are born. Membership in the church does not only include older people who have said they wish to follow Jesus, but also their children. These children are often referred to as "children of the covenant."

If a person has been baptized or confirmed in another church, that person will be warmly received into the Presbyterian Church as a brother or sister in Christ. This is because Presbyterians baptize people into the universal church in the name of the Father, Son, and Holy Spirit. They are baptized into the Christian church, not the Presbyterian Church. Presbyterians recognize the baptismal rites of other Christian denominations as legitimate.

Presbyterians believe that a person should be baptized only once and, as a result, are very much opposed to any form of re-baptism. An exception would be if a person has forgotten or does not know whether or not they have been baptized. In that case, the minister will baptize the person saying it is being done on the condition the person has not already been baptized.

If, however, an adult wishes to join who has never become a member in any Christian denomination, they will be received by "believer's baptism," confessing their faith at the same time they are baptized. In my own case, because I came from the Baptist tradition which believes only in baptizing persons who are old enough to understand and confess their faith, I had not been baptized as a child. As a result, when I confessed my faith I was also baptized. Likewise, people who have not been raised in a Christian home and wish to enter the Christian faith will also be baptized as adults in the Presbyterian Church at the same time as they profess their faith.

I have come to believe that infant baptism better conveys the meaning of God's love than anything else we do in the church. Will Campbell, renegade Baptist preacher in Tennessee, was asked to baptize the three-year-old son of his daughter. Fearing what his lifelong, Baptist, deacon father might think, Will asked him if he believed in infant baptism. "Believe in it," scoffed his father, "I've actually seen it!"

Infant baptism dramatically displays that, before the child can become aware of God, God claims the child as a member of God's family. Before the child can seek to please God, God seeks and accepts the child. But what is so clearly seen in infant baptism is, in reality, true for us all. God loves, accepts, and forgives us before we offer anything to God.

Communion

While Presbyterians believe baptism is a one-time event, the Lord's Supper or communion occurs many times. Through this means, God nurtures and sustains people.

What actually happens during communion? Usually communion is set in the midst of a worship service after the reading of scripture and the sermon. The central act of communion occurs when bread is broken and it, along with wine, is distributed among the worshipers who are urged to remember the death and suffering of Jesus and to celebrate God's presence with them now. At one time, Presbyterians used a common cup and fermented wine. Due to health concerns and in deference to those who may be addicted to alcohol, many Presbyterians now use grape juice and individual cups which are passed to the worshipers in their pews.

You may encounter a number of other practices in Presbyterian churches. You may be asked to come forward to the table to receive the elements or, in small gatherings, all may sit around the table for the whole service. Many churches prepare the bread beforehand into small cubes. Mainly, I suspect, this is done for the convenience of the worshiper. More congregations have returned to providing a loaf of bread from which each worshiper breaks a piece. The idea is that a loaf of bread better symbolizes the one body of Christ from which we are all fed.

In some congregations, when you arrive for the communion service, you will find the elements already spread out on the communion table. Frequently they will be covered by a white linen cloth which is removed by the elders just before the service of communion begins. Other congregations find it more meaningful to have the elements carried in in a processional, thereby symbolizing that these are the gifts of the people to be dedicated and used in the service.

Usually, it will be the elders who, having been served the communion by the minister, will then distribute it among the people. But there is nothing to prevent other people from serving. In congregations I pastored, we often invited the young people to participate in this way.

Variations also occur in the order of serving. Some believe it is more scriptural for the minister to eat and drink first, as Jesus did in the account in the Bible. Others feel it is more appropriate that the minister eat and drink last, thereby better portraying the image of the Christian as servant.

Next time you attend communion, try to observe the various practices in your congregation. You may wish to discuss the reason for the way things are done with your minister or elder.

My own earliest memory of the sacrament was the time when some young boys drank all of the grape juice before the service. The deacons rushed to the local corner store and that morning we used grape pop.

I grew up in a tradition which viewed communion primarily as a time to remember the life and death of Christ. For Presbyterians too, communion involves remembering. But more than that, it is a holy and even mystical event, although no magic is involved. The sacrament helps us in our living in ways we don't fully comprehend. Jesus is present in the sacrament, but not in a literal or mechanical way.

A few years ago, Peter Gzowski wrote a book about a small plane which crashed in the mountains. On board were a father, his daughter, her brother-in-law, and the pilot. The father and pilot died in the crash. A small fire occurred when the plane crashed and a part of the father's leg had been literally cooked. In order to survive, the daughter and brother-in-law ate this flesh. Gzowski called this difficult but gripping story *The Sacrament*.

Presbyterians do not believe that they actually eat the flesh of Jesus, but they do believe that the sacrament provides life for them just as surely as it did for the people in the plane crash.

In the Anglican tradition, emphasis is placed on communion as a meal to strengthen the body of Christ. Logic decrees, therefore, that the more frequently you celebrate communion the better.

Traditionally, in Presbyterian churches, the sacrament is only celebrated four times a year. That should not be taken as a sign that Presbyterians take the sacrament less seriously, however. In the Scottish tradition, people were involved in a long period of preparation before taking the sacrament. Because of great distances and long traveling times, this preparation involved many weeks. Members were called upon to examine their lives carefully to ensure, in Saint Paul's words, they did not eat and drink to their own damnation.

Two things from that era survive in some Presbyterian churches today. One is a Preparatory Service, often held on the Friday evening before Sunday communion. Special emphasis in this service is laid on preparing oneself to receive communion.

The other is the communion card or token. In the early days in Scotland, after the elder or minister had visited a family and was convinced they were in a proper spiritual condition to receive the sacrament, the family was given a communion token. These were originally made of metal with the initials of the minister or the name of the congregation imprinted on them. On some, an appropriate verse from scripture such as, "This do in remembrance of me," was also imprinted on the small coin. This token then became their proof of their fitness to receive communion and would be collected at church on communion Sunday.

Today elders still visit their members before communion. In

place of a metal token, members are given small cards. These cards are then brought to worship on communion Sunday. Some people jokingly refer to the elders as "ecclesiastical postmen or women," but the practice does ensure regular visitation of people, and it provides a means of maintaining a record of communion attendance.

Many congregations feel the need to move to more frequent celebrations of the sacrament in accordance with Calvin's wishes. In the last congregation I served, we celebrated eight times yearly, four of which were declared card-carrying communions. In other words, only on quarterly communions did elders deliver communion cards.

A few years ago the General Assembly gave permission for young children not yet confirmed as members to receive communion. As a prerequisite to participation, their parents must give permission and the children themselves receive instruction appropriate to their own age level.

The church provides materials to be used for instruction with children. The first time I used this material with young children, they, including my own son, astounded me with their depth of understanding. Much of this knowledge had been picked up through observation. But also, children often can appreciate aspects of a subject conveyed through drama, play, and the senses to which adults are less sensitive. A keen mind is not the sole prerequisite for learning, especially when it comes to subjects such as the Lord's Supper.

For you...

Nothing reflects better what Presbyterians believe about the sacraments than these words which are taken from the order of worship for baptism in the Reformed Church in France. The pastor speaks to the infant about to be baptized:

> Little child, for you Jesus Christ came into the world, he suffered; for you he went through the agony of Gethsemane and the darkness of Calvary; for you he cried 'It is finished'; for you he triumphed over death... For you, and you, little child, do not yet know anything about this. But thus is the statement of the apostle confirmed, 'We love God because he first loved us.'"

Chapter 10

Canairelief flies in relief supplies during Nigerian civil war.

Photos: *Presbyterian Record*

Scott Mission

Moderator George Vais presents the church's confession to Grand Chief Phil Fontaine as Kay Cowper, president of the WMS, looks on.

The family acts: the church and social action

The Spirit of the Lord is upon me,
because he has anointed me
to preach good news to the poor.
He has sent me
to proclaim release to the captives
and recovering of sight to the blind,
to set at liberty
those who are oppressed,
to proclaim
the acceptable year of the Lord.
—Jesus, Luke 4:16–19 RSV

Never before had I been called a communist or been spat upon. But the day I walked in a parade to protest the war in Vietnam it happened.

The decision to participate hadn't been an easy one to make. I didn't want to be in that march, but I felt I had to be. I had read everything I could on the war. I had attended seminars and listened to theologians and others reflect on it. I had talked to a Vietnamese student who was studying in Canada. Ultimately, I had concluded that the war was a mistake and that the church should speak out against it.

Most of the people in the pew were not prepared for this. Why should they be? The church in the first half of the century concerned itself primarily with issues of booze and Sabbath observance. When I tried to discuss the Vietnam war in the session of the small inner-city congregation I served, only one member thought it worth consideration.

Despite this, when the protest walk was proposed, I felt I should participate. True, I cowered in the midst of some Mennonite friends; as pacifists, I reasoned they were used to this kind of thing. But at least I went.

During the previous decade, Presbyterians had gone to Selma, Alabama, to walk in solidarity with Martin Luther King. These two events, the civil rights struggle in the United States and the Vietnam war, drew many Christians into the struggle for justice in the world.

If a commissioner to General Assembly 50 years ago could attend an Assembly today, he or she would scarcely be able to comprehend the vast number of social issues being grappled with by the church. In 1994, those issues represented every area of life. The Assembly's pronouncements on economic matters would have stunned someone attending a half century earlier. Recommendations regarding trade and trading agreements designed to assist smaller countries were directed to the Government of Canada. The Assembly also requested that the government work to cancel or reschedule debts owed by countries in the Southern Hemisphere, and that the criteria for eligibility for international credit be supplemented by considerations of social justice, human rights, and democratic participation.

The Assembly requested that the federal government shorten the period of patent protection for pharmaceutical drugs, which was passed in 1993. Cheaper drugs, it declared, would mean health care for people who could not otherwise afford it. The Assembly asked its finance committee to increase the Presbyterian Church's contribution to the Economic Development Cooperative Society in 1995. This organization provides loans for cooperative, self-development enterprises that cannot secure funding through the usual lending organizations.

Motions were adopted regarding the world's trouble spots, such as South Africa and the Middle East. A statement on the "Theology of Peacemaking" declared that "God does not glorify our wars, nor allow us to take joy and satisfaction freely from defeating our enemy." Moreover, it calls on all Christians to work for a just and peaceful society.

Fifty years ago, commissioners could not have envisioned the long debate over the Report on Human Sexuality, which urged support for traditional Christian and moral values, but also delved into areas of homosexuality and masturbation.

Also in 1994, a significant step regarding our church's relationship with aboriginal peoples was taken at the General Assembly, when the church adopted "The 1994 Confession of The Presbyterian Church in Canada Regarding Injustice Suffered by Canada's First Nation Peoples."

The Presbyterian Church had operated two residential schools. The confession acknowledges that the Presbyterian Church cooperated with the government of Canada to assimilate aboriginal people. Although many members of the church gave themselves in love and compassion on behalf of aboriginal brothers and sisters, the confession also admits to the church's cultural arrogance in believing it knew better than the aboriginal people what they needed. The confession acknowledges our church's role in residential schools, where children were deprived of their traditional ways and customs, where disciplinary practices were used which were unknown to aboriginal peoples, and where students were exploited with physical and psychological punishment beyond natural care and discipline.

The confession acknowledges that lives have been deeply scarred by the effects of this mission and asks for the forgiveness of both God and the aboriginal people. It concludes: "With God's guidance, our church will seek opportunities to walk with aboriginal peoples to find healing and wholeness together as

God's people."

In October 1994, this process was begun when the Moderator visited Winnipeg and presented the confession to Grand Chief Phil Fontaine and other leaders of the First Nations.

Although all the courts of the church can pronounce on social issues, most of this work is done by the General Assembly and its agencies (staff and committees). Today it would be difficult to uncover a social issue that the Assembly has not made a statement about, urged governmental action on, or asked its membership to address.

You may purchase a social action manual which lists all of the statements on social issues made by the Presbyterian Church over the years. Available from the Resources and Communications department the initial cost of the manual also includes yearly updates.

Maintaining personal morality

For most of us, this broad concern for the social welfare of the global community has become so commonplace that we assume it has always been that way. Not so. For much of its life, social action was seen primarily in terms of maintaining personal morality. Irving Layton's well-known comment on this theme is typical: "What luck, what luck to be loved by the one girl in this Presbyterian country who knows how to give a man pleasure."

Partly this was the result of the tremendous influence of the Free Church of Scotland on the early development of the Canadian church. In 1843 in Scotland, the Presbyterian Church divided over the issue of its relationship to the state and how much influence the government should have in church affairs. The Free Church took the position that the state should exert no influence in appointing the church's leaders or directing its policy. As a result, a strong sentiment for the separation of church and state developed in the Free Church. This carried over into Canada where the Free Church was active in missionary endeavors and where even those associated with the Church of Scotland seemed sympathetic to the Free Church view. This, despite the fact that in Canada the whole issue was irrelevant because there was no state-supported church.

Over the years, the issue which most consumed Presbyterians

was Sabbath day observance. Presbyterians believed in strict observance. The day should be given over to worship, teaching, and prayer. No work nor recreational activity was allowed.

A friend of mine, whose father was a Presbyterian minister, remembers a time in the 1920s when his father made some young boys stop playing baseball because it was Sunday. My friend's father then went home and listened to the Detroit Tigers game. It was something, my friend says, he understood neither then nor now.

Rev. D. James Macdonnell was serving St. Andrew's Church in Toronto in 1883. The story goes that he was once visiting his father-in-law, the Rev. George Smellie, the Free Church minister of Melville Church in Fergus, Ontario. A contemporary, J. S. Macdonnell, tells the story in a memoir.

> On Sunday afternoon, the children being at Sunday school, the grown-ups repaired to the orchard to sing hymns. I am sure that my parents and uncles and aunts, long away from the parental roof, were of the opinion that such engagement would meet with approval in the high place; but what was their consternation when my grandfather emerged from the house, and bade them in stern tones to stop their profane singing, as it was evident they were singing for their own pleasure, and not for the glory of God.

Little wonder that such strict application of the Ten Commandments, and particularly the one about keeping the Sabbath day holy, has led many modern folk to think of Presbyterians as a rather dour and melancholy group.

The validity of the complaint that Presbyterianism sought to throw a wet blanket of strict morality over the country can be justified when viewed through Presbyterian involvement in the Lord's Day Alliance which was founded in Ottawa in 1888. Principal William Caven of Knox College headed the Ontario Lord's Day Alliance. Rev. W.D. Armstrong, a Presbyterian, presided over the national organization. Half of the executive were Presbyterians.

Not so, however, when it came to prohibition, the other consuming interest of the church in Canada in the first half of the 20th century. Here the Methodists took the lead and Presbyterians played a supporting and sometimes hesitant role. Presbyterians are frequently associated with Scotch whisky, but no such jokes are ever attributed to Methodists.

A typical story of this kind is told of the Presbyterian minister in Glasgow who met an elder who was obviously "the worse for wear." The minister asked the elder what he was doing in this disgraceful condition.

"I am delivering communion tokens," he said. The minister enquired how this fact explained the elder's inebriation.

"The people offer me 'a wee dramie' and, of course, I must be polite and accept."

"Does everyone in your district offer you a drink?"

"No, but if they don't, I just mail the communion token."

In 1893, when the governments of Prince Edward Island and Ontario proposed a plebiscite on the question of prohibition, the *Presbyterian Record* laid out the pros and cons of the issue, but took no position itself nor offered any advice. That would not have been the case on questions regarding Sabbath observance.

I experienced this difference as a child in the 1940s and '50s. Students in the United Church Sunday school were asked to sign pledge cards indicating they would never imbibe alcoholic beverages. That never happened in the Presbyterian Sunday School despite the fact that Presbyterians were more conservative theologically than their United Church friends. When I enquired why we had not been asked to take the pledge, I was told that the official position of the Presbyterian Church was moderation, not abstinence.

Although it has taken a strong stand on the importance of education regarding alcohol, and the dangers of alcohol advertising (which the General Assembly has asked to have banned on a number of occasions), the Assembly has always maintained an official stance of moderation. In 1950 it produced a statement enunciating this policy, and in 1976 reaffirmed it.

This does not mean that the Presbyterian Church had no social conscience before modern times. It is important to keep in mind that individual Christians have always served on the front lines of social concern, even though their activity may not have been under direct church sponsorship.

Early prophets of social reform included Rev. James Robertson, who exhibited a concern for the primitive living conditions in the West. Rev. John Shearer fought against the vices being bred in the new cities.

Shearer played a leading role at a Pre-Assembly Congress in 1913 in Massey Hall. Among the resolutions passed, one stated that all parts of the church should "immediately unite in facing the 'situation in Canada, so unprecedented and so urgent' by working toward the 'humanizing and Christianizing' of the social, industrial, civic aspects of Canadian life."

In response, the Assembly that year urged all Presbyterians to study these problems and work toward solving them.

Rev. C. W. Gordon helped the church create the Committee on Temperance and Moral Reform in 1907. And Rev. George Grant founded the Good Samaritan Hospital in Dawson City during the gold rush. As well, he was a leading member of the Moral and Social Reform League.

The Presbyterian Church might have continued to develop a strong social conscience had not the Church Union controversy of 1925 intervened. That year, two-thirds of the Presbyterian Church joined with the Methodists and Congregationalists to form the United Church of Canada. More than two-thirds of the clergy entered the union. As a result, for many years after 1925, the Presbyterian Church became obsessed with its own survival and reconstruction, to the exclusion of almost everything else. As well, most of the leaders in social reform in the Presbyterian Church had entered the Union. James Mutchmor, who became a high profile United Church leader addressing social issues in the '50s, had been a former Presbyterian.

In 1933, the General Assembly established a special committee on Evangelism and Church Life and Work, which became a permanent committee of the Assembly the following year. However, it dealt mainly with social issues affecting individual morals, such as alcohol, gambling, pornography, Sabbath observance, and motion picture censorship. In 1935, in the midst of the Great Depression, the committee proclaimed: "the greatest social and economic need of today is the protection and proper use of the Lord's Day."

Response to the great social evils of the day mainly took the form of relief work. During this period the Scott Mission, under a converted Jew, Alex Zeidman, was established in Toronto. But again, it was not so much the church as a whole acting as it was the response of one individual who had been touched by the terrible hunger and need of those around him.

Rising awareness

What happened to so radically change the approach and emphasis of the Presbyterian Church in dealing with social issues? What made it turn its face towards evil and address it as it manifested itself in the structures of society?

The Second World War for one thing. The rise of Hitler and the capitulation of much of the church in the face of this great evil made the Canadian church realize this was an area it could no longer neglect. The rise of justice movements in the United States, especially relating to the race issue, also helped to motivate our church to greater action.

In 1942, Gordon Peddie, a parish minister, published a book entitled *The King of Kings*. He wrote it in support of the Presbytery of Paris's request that the church clarify its standards in relationship to Christ's lordship over the nations and their rulers. The problem, Peddie believed, was that the church was confessionless on the church's relationship to the civil state. Presbyterians believed that Jesus Christ was Lord over all of life, but their confessions failed to signify this. As a result, the church had fallen into a state of silence and inaction on social issues.

Perhaps no single individual had a greater influence on bringing about this change than did Allan Farris, who for many years taught Church History at Knox College. "It is a terrible parody of the gospel," he wrote in the October 1959 issue of the *Presbyterian Record*, "to talk about the love of God and then fail to relate it to the dreadful agony that millions of men and women experience in this world."

Farris was a popular preacher in the evangelical tradition and therefore acceptable to the mainline of the church. He sought, through his teaching and preaching, to recover and reassert John Calvin's teaching that Christ's lordship should extend to both the church and the world.

Between 1959 and 1974 Farris wrote three articles for the

Presbyterian Record on the theme of the church's social responsibility. These articles reflect not only the evolution and development of his own thought on this issue, but also the change that took place in the mind of the church. Farris affected a whole generation of students who became leaders in the church.

In October 1959, Farris reported on a conference he attended in northern Greece. At the conference, 120 delegates from 34 countries discussed Christian responsibility in the light of rapid social change. The action he suggested the church should take hardly seems radical today, but for many in 1959 it was: speak out in prophetic anger against exploitation, encourage members to engage in responsible political action, and support all organizations (even those not Christian) which promote human welfare.

Symbolically, on the next page of the same issue, an article appeared by the young theologian Joseph McLelland. McLelland, a friend and student of Farris, declared: "Surely the church must help its people to replace the virtue of personal charity with the demand of social justice." McLelland would go on to be a leader in this revolution, both as a popular conference speaker, and with his ability to communicate with the laity through his writings, such as his book *The Other Six Days.*

In the April 1966 issue of the *Record*, Farris advanced and enlarged his thesis concerning social action by declaring that "Any gospel...which lacks a social dimension is not true to the teaching of the Bible." He concluded with an even stronger statement and question: "...Christ gave himself in total commitment to the whole range of human needs... Dare we, who claim to be biblical Christians, put to the periphery what God by intent and design has placed in the very center of his redemptive acts?"

In May 1974, he wrote an article entitled "John Calvin, Social Revolutionary." In it we see where much of Farris's thought and inspiration originated. He declared that "The church for Calvin was a kind of 'pilot project' of a restored and renewed community. That was why it was so important for the Christian church to engage in serious social service and to be the vanguard for the realization of social justice."

Farris showed how Calvin lashed out against hoarders and wheat-cornering operators, whom Calvin described as "murderers, savage beasts, biting and eating up the poor, sucking up their blood."

"A Calvinist," Farris concluded, "if true to Calvin, will be a social reformer, a compassionate advocate of justice for all, and an implacable foe of tyranny..."

I graduated from Knox College in 1962 after three years under Farris's tutelage and that of other professors such as Donald Wade, who held similar views on social action. I often say that when I graduated I really did not have a clear idea what I should do in the world, but I had no doubt that the Christian message should somehow be brought to bear on the everyday issues affecting the lives of people.

In my third year in my first parish in Biggar, Saskatchewan, the *Saskatoon Star Phoenix* carried an editorial cartoon showing a little man with a briefcase standing beside a train engine. The engineer scratches his head while looking at this person and asks, "What kind of minister is this?"

The cartoon had been inspired by my appearance the previous day before the Friedman Royal Commission on the question of railway run-throughs in the West. Run-throughs were decisions taken by the railway to no longer change crews at certain points. By changing crews less frequently the railway believed they could save a great deal of money. But in doing this, they required their staff to work longer hours and in the process destroyed many prairie towns. To settle the dispute the federal government appointed a one-person commission, Justice Friedman of the Manitoba Supreme Court, to settle the dispute.

Inspired by people such as Allan Farris, I had traveled in engines and cabooses with members of my congregation on their regular routes to gain some understanding of their work. I persuaded the Biggar Ministerial to make a submission from the point of view of the workers and residents of Biggar. Somewhat reluctantly, they agreed if I would both write and make the submission, which I did. I remember vividly the consternation of the lawyer for the railway, a Presbyterian from Montreal, who felt the church, and especially its clergy, had no business interfering in railway matters. From his experience of the lack of involvement by our church in social issues, his dismay was understandable.

Social action and evangelism

As interest in social issues rapidly escalated, many in the church feared the cause of evangelism might be lost. Allan Farris would not have had the same impact in the church had he not also been a passionate defender and advocate of the gospel in terms of the need of personal repentance and conversion.

The Presbyterian Church has always struggled to keep its concern for evangelism and social action balanced, as this statement by the 1968 General Assembly indicates:

> Evangelism and Christian Social Action though not identical are inseparably related because both adhere to, and are indispensable parts of, the Gospel of Jesus Christ... Wherever the Church begins to ignore one to the exclusion of the other amounts to nothing less than a distortion of the Gospel.

Farris also played a significant role in the drafting and ultimate adoption by the General Assembly in 1955 of the *Declaration of Faith Concerning Church and Nation*. This declaration provided the theoretical and theological framework which Presbyterians always require before engaging in any action.

Arthur Gowland also deserves much credit for the evolving social conscience of Presbyterians.

In 1945, the committee on Evangelism and Church Life and Work changed its name to the Board of Evangelism and Social Action. It began a search for a full-time secretary. Finally, in 1959, a minister from Toronto, Arthur Gowland, was appointed.

Two things made Gowland effective. Like Farris, he was seen to be in the mainstream of the Presbyterian Church. The term "radical" simply did not fit his image. His other quality suited to the job was tenacity. He did not discourage easily. Year after year he would pound away at social issues until action was forthcoming.

With a full-time secretary, the board now had the time and resources to consider a wide range of social issues. To show the importance of this appointment, in 1960, only one year after he began, the report of the Board of Evangelism and Social Action addressed the following issues: penal reform, nuclear weapons, racial discrimination in public housing and immigration, Canadian Indians and antisemitism.

Discussion and statements on other issues soon followed:

drugs, automation, union security and the right to work, euthanasia, homosexuality, and ecology.

The rise of various church coalitions paralleled this concern to address evil manifested in the social structures of society, and aided in the struggle against it.

Churches of all denominations began to ask themselves what they could do together about these issues. From the beginning, Presbyterians made a contribution which far exceeded their numbers in personnel, if not in dollars. Because of the limited size of the Presbyterian staff many lay persons became heavily involved representing the Presbyterian Church on these coalitions.

An example of the importance with which others viewed the Presbyterian contribution occurred early in the 1980s. The Presbyterian Church decided to withdraw from Ten Days for World Development, a church umbrella which promoted world service and relief in all the denominations. Presbyterians felt that Ten Days was not doing the job and that therefore they could not financially support it. However, the other partners urged us to stay on even if it meant giving no financial support to the program.

The church coalitions got a huge boost in the wake of Vatican II when Roman Catholics began to join and support them.

One of the first coalitions was PLURA, a provincially administered organization, which financed self-help programs throughout Canada. Projects included music programs and efforts to respond to physically challenged persons. The name PLURA is formed from the first letters of the sponsoring denominations: Presbyterian, Lutheran, United, Roman Catholic and Anglican.

As mentioned earlier, Ten Days for World Development developed as a coalition to promote and educate Canadians on what the churches did in world service overseas. Leaders of the churches, including the Presbyterian Moderator, toured Canada speaking about the work.

Gatt-Fly, now the Ecumenical Coalition on Economic Justice, was headed by a Presbyterian, Geoffrey Johnston, for 10 years. Brian Fraser played a major role in the formation of the Task Force of Churches on Corporate Responsibility, which sought to make large corporations become ethically responsible in their investments and dealings in other countries. And Charles Hay, former principal of Knox College, became a major player with the Interchurch Coalition on Refugees. The Canada China program, begun in 1963 to foster understanding of China and assist the church there, was initiated by Ted Johnson who at the time served as Overseas Secretary of the Board of World Mission of the Presbyterian Church.

By 1983, Presbyterian World Service listed 12 different coalitions in which the Presbyterian Church participated.

The value of these coalitions, according to Marjorie Ross, a veteran of work with coalitions and now head of International Ministries, is that together the churches can do research and advocacy which would be impossible for most of them on their own.

Do Presbyterians take a different approach to social issues than other denominations? Some would argue no, they are just slower reacting and getting involved than other denominations. What the United Church is dealing with today the Presbyterians will get around to in about ten years.

Not so, says Ray Hodgson, who today heads up Justice Ministries for the Presbyterian Church. The reason we seem slow is that Presbyterians insist on doing their theological homework before taking action. Presbyterians insist that theology precedes action.

As I mentioned in chapter seven, I saw this happen in a practical way in my own congregation in North York. The congregation built a housing project which was attached to the church. The 70-unit project included single-parent families as well as physically challenged young people who needed attendant care. Projects such as this, in which a congregation works in partnership with the government, are common among Presbyterian congregations as in most other denominations. But what intrigued me about our project was that it all seemed to start with a stewardship question. Did we have the right before God to use only 12 percent of our land when there was such a great need for special housing all around us?

The congregation responded to the challenge magnificently, despite militant opposition from some in the community who felt it would threaten their land values and bring “undesirables” into their community.

Nor could I envision in the 1960s that 20 years later my congregation would sponsor several families of Vietnam refugees, assisting them to settle in Canada and integrate into Canadian life.

This came about as the result of an agreement between various denominations, including ours, and the federal government to allow churches to sponsor refugees. The congregation enthusiastically embraced this opportunity as a response to the biblical call to help the poor, the needy, and the refugee.

Naturally, not all members are happy with the church's social involvement. Even those who are happy with such involvement are not always pleased with what the church says and does. Today the church wrestles with how it will treat its members of homosexual orientation, an issue which has the potential to deeply divide its membership. But the church has faced similar difficult issues in the past and has survived.

Not long ago, support for so-called revolutionary groups in Africa caused much debate. The day on which I write this, Nelson Mandela has been elected as the new Prime Minister of South Africa. Most Christians, at least in retrospect, are pleased that the church played an important part, not only in Mandela's release from prison and his rise to power, but in freedom coming to South Africa.

If at some time you are a dissenter to a decision or action taken by the church, as I have been on occasion, remember it's not the Devil that makes Christians get involved in social action, it's John Calvin. And before him Jesus Christ. And before Jesus, Moses and the prophets.

In their report to the General Assembly in 1966, the Board of Evangelism and Social Action put it well:

> ...Christian Social Action is not simply a hobby of the church that we can play if we happen to have time, and can ignore with impunity. It is an integral part of the Gospel of Jesus Christ, and therefore any attempt to be neutral to the social issues and challenges of the world today, is not only to close our eyes to the many hundreds of passages in the Bible devoted to social responsibility, it is also to fail to understand the nature and scope of the glorious Gospel of Jesus Christ that the church is under orders to proclaim.

Stuart McDonald, a young minister in our church, recalls how this insight became real to him.

> There were about 25 of us. Amid skyscrapers that housed

dealers in power and wealth, we gathered outside the South African consulate and called for an end to apartheid. Tourists stared, puzzled. Business people gave jaded glances. Counter-demonstrators looked with hostility. There I was, following Jesus. It was one of the first times I publicly put what I believed on the line and stood up for justice because I followed Jesus Christ. It wasn't easy. To say something different, to speak of justice and love to a world that isn't sure what either means—that is what being a follower of Jesus is all about.

Chapter 11

Photo: *Presbyterian Record*

First Atlantic Cursillo: Alex MacDonald (R) Scott Johnston (L).

Being Presbyterian today and tomorrow: the family reaches out

> "to repent, not whimper"... to examine critically its tradition, discarding the trash, while confidently affirming the treasure. Perhaps, just perhaps, God will choose to use these efforts to revitalize God's mainline witnesses.
>
> —Leander Keck

Hardly a day passes without a new prediction that mainline Protestants, like Presbyterians, are on their way out. Indeed, our numerical decline since the 1960s gives credence to the possibility that when we enter the 21st century there may no longer be a mainline Presbyterian witness in Canada. In 1960, there were almost 200,000 members on the roles of our congregations. By the 1990s, that number had declined to approximately 150,000.

Ironically this decline, until the last two years, has not affected the generosity of Presbyterians whose givings to the national budget (Presbyterians Sharing) have increased, although not as much percentage-wise as givings for congregational purposes. The budget for the national church, which includes support for missions in Canada and overseas, Christian education, pensions, and theological education, is in excess of nine and one half million dollars.

In one sense, whether or not Presbyterianism survives is not the critical issue. What is important is whether or not the Church of Jesus Christ survives in a credible form. The survival of Presbyterianism is only significant to the degree that we have a faithful contribution to make to that one, universal Church of God.

If you agree with me that we **do** have an important role to play in Canada, the question becomes one of how we can play it with effectiveness and relevance.

Over the past few years, much of the energy of our denomination has been consumed in a revisioning process which resulted in a new nine-point vision (see Appendix, pg. 159) being formulated and adopted by our denomination. Among its objectives are the integration of evangelism, social action and justice ministry, and the commitment to become a loving, inclusive community.

In its wake came proposals for radical structural change. The many departments of the denomination became two agencies—Service, and Life and Mission. This change was a response to the vision statement that administration should become lean and accountable, and was an effort to enable the denomination to work more cooperatively and effectively.

No doubt the change was also a response to an aging and declining denomination with the hope that such a reorganization might help to stem the decline. In *Fragmented Gods*, Reginald Bibby noted that older Presbyterians represent one-third of the church and that, as a denomination, we will lose a greater proportion of our members and adherents through death than most other denominations. Although he was working with "census Presbyterians," not actual communicant members, and census figures nearly ten years old, the truth of what Bibby described cannot be denied. Indeed, recent census figures have painted an even bleaker picture. New immigrants from areas of the world in which Presbyterianism is particularly strong, such as Guyana and Korea, provide one glimmer of hope here.

Unfortunately, as a denomination, we have yet to become effective in outreach (evangelism) aimed at attracting younger persons to the church. During its existence in Canada, the Presbyterian Church has survived and flourished mainly through the continual supply of new Presbyterian immigrants who have arrived on our shores, especially from Scotland and Ireland. Perhaps because of this, we have forgotten or failed to develop our ability to share our own stories and faith, and to be an open and inviting church for outsiders.

Compounding this problem is the fact that we continue to lose approximately 50 percent of the children we baptize—that is, they fail to make a profession of faith and become active in the Presbyterian Church. It will be important for both local congregations as well as the institution to focus resources on these issues.

Reclaiming our core commitments

There are signs this may already be happening. In 1994, the Life and Mission Agency called upon the church to make "face-to-face evangelism" the emphasis in our denomination for the next five years. The agency hopes that this kind of evangelism, "conducted at a personal or relational level, individually and in small groups," will remove preconceived ideas, as well as the fear and guilt that Presbyterians often have around the subject of evangelism. In carrying out workshops, the Education for Discipleship team will make this kind of evangelism a part of every workshop.

One of the best examples of this kind of evangelism I know of was done by a young engineer in a congregation I served. The story he told was simple. When someone new arrived at his place of employment, he invited them to come with him to worship next Sunday. "I find something important there for me," he would tell them, "and I think you would too." He introduced more people to our congregation and faith than anyone I have ever met. In the process, he illustrated the best definition of evangelism I have ever heard: "one beggar telling another where to get food."

Within Presbyterianism, God still provides food and drink for hungry travelers. Presbyterians will thrive as they share what

God provides.

The 1925 Church Union left few Presbyterians in some parts of the country. This was particularly true in the West. As a result, today the great majority of Presbyterians live in southern Ontario—Guelph is the geographical center of Presbyterianism. In maintaining a sense of identity and representation across Canada, the Presbyterian Church faces some of the same problems that bedevil many of our political parties.

But beyond all of these issues, in an age of relativism in which every philosophy or religion is considered equally valid, the Presbyterian Church must state, with enthusiasm and conviction, what we believe about Jesus Christ. Kenneth McMillan, former general secretary of the Canadian Bible Society, correctly contends that the vitality of any church is historically tied to its attitude to Jesus Christ. Denominational rhetoric regularly celebrates our diversity, often forgetting that, by itself, the celebration of diversity can be little more than an exercise in fragmentation.

We also need to recover our confidence as a denomination in a specifically Reformed view and vision of the church and life. The purpose of this book is to help in that process. Some have criticized the vision statement as being a document which any Christian could easily affirm. That in itself is not necessarily a bad thing, as long as we move on from there to articulate the particular Reformed and Presbyterian view of reality.

That vision would of necessity include an emphasis on the "otherness" or sovereignty of God. David Hay, former professor of Knox College and tireless worker in the ecumenical movement, has described this Presbyterian vision as "the vision of the glory of God." Some Christians, he writes, "rest their confidence upon the subjective experience of conversion. Presbyterians rest on something much, much stronger—the electing grace of God." This emphasis, Hay believes, if recovered properly in the church, could strike at the heart of the two chief factors diminishing the influence of the church today—secularism and self-interest.

Having said that, we need to recognize that the real life of any denomination will be found in the local congregation. I like the way Harris Kirk, minister of Franklin Street Presbyterian Church in Baltimore through the first half of this century, put it. The power to change the direction of the world, Kirk said, will not come from "general deliverances of church councils," nor from "proclamations made within the region of religious platitudes," but "from multitudes of nameless folk, who lived wholesome, believing lives, who endeavored honestly to carry out the will of Christ in their private and public life, and who rest today in unvisited tombs."

Doing old things well

During my six years as editor of the *Presbyterian Record* I have had the opportunity to visit many Presbyterian congregations throughout Canada. Some are struggling to survive. Many others, however, would not know what you were talking about if you told them that the mainline denominations were dying. That is not their experience. Their congregations continue as lively, involved, and often growing fellowships of Christians. I have often asked myself what makes the difference between the vibrant groups, and those congregations staring death in the face.

Many factors are involved, such as location and demographic changes in the area in which the congregation is located. But beyond that, I have concluded the most important factors involve leadership and the ability to do the old things well.

The minister does not have to be Billy Graham. But in Presbyterian congregations, he or she needs to expound the Bible faithfully, visit the congregation regularly, and pray. The elders need to be deeply committed and work cooperatively and harmoniously with the minister in all aspects of the church's work. In most cases, when that happens, the congregation will remain viable.

A key word for all congregations today is flexibility. Within the basic structures I have mentioned above, and responding to the historic strengths of the Reformed faith, how should the shape and mission of the local congregation develop today?

In a pluralistic society, many people call for Christians to work with non-Christians in confronting common issues and concerns. A natural area of concern for Presbyterians, who have traditionally emphasized the role of God as creator, will be environmental issues.

Bob Killey a member of St. Mark's in North York, Ontario, believed that he could "reap a groundswell of people who want to do something positive for the environment." He started his own non-profit organization called, We Can Make A Difference. He sells what he describes as "products of conscience" through young people's groups in churches. The young people reap a small financial benefit for their group, but Killey emphasizes that this is "not the primary purpose of the program; it is a stewardship program to save the earth."

Living every day before God

From a Presbyterian or Reformed perspective, all of life must be lived out before God. Divisions between the religious and secular are false. Presbyterians are well placed, therefore, to respond to the demand that congregations challenge the issues which face the everyday lives of people today.

Presbyterian congregations are confronting AIDS, through education and by ministering to those suffering from the disease. After posing the question, "If Christ walked on earth now and tested HIV positive, would we visit him?" St. Andrew's in Calgary launched a thorough AIDS education and action program using not only people in their own congregation, but also experts from the public sector. This resulted, not only in people being better educated about AIDS, but in new volunteers at AIDS Calgary, and a greater bond with and acceptance of those suffering from AIDS.

In February 1992, the Supreme Court of Canada ruled unanimously that our country's laws against pornography are both legitimate and necessary. This proceeding launched Carolyn Keith of Westwood Church, Winnipeg, into action. She mobilized a community group called GAP (Group Against Pornography) that has successfully stopped the proliferation of adult video stores in Winnipeg and throughout Manitoba.

Only recently has society become aware of the terrible ravages of sexual abuse. Responding to this, Elmwood Presbyterian in London, Ontario, has begun to minister to survivors of sexual abuse. A support group has been formed using the resources of their minister as well as those provided through the Inter-Faith Christian Counseling Center.

Putting faith into action

Reformed Christians have always believed in putting their faith into action. Remember the person who said he would rather meet an army with fixed bayonets than one Calvinist who believed he was doing God's will? That fits nicely with the present age in which actions increasingly take precedence over words. Presbyterian congregations will need to respond to this challenge.

In 1992, John Tollenaar, a young farmer who lives near Monkton, Ontario, got the idea that, although rural churches had declined in size and numbers, their desire to serve God had not. Why couldn't the members in his church, he wondered, grow 50 acres of corn for the Canadian Foodgrains Bank to help feed the starving of the world? The farmers would purchase seed; they would fertilize, till, plant, and harvest the crop. Partners in city churches could participate by contributing to the financial cost of about $13,000. People responded enthusiastically. The idea has now spread to several other congregations. In 1993, 215 metric tonnes of corn were donated to the Canadian Foodgrains Bank.

Although some congregations have experienced a decline in givings, many still have large financial reserves. Congregations need to use these in more imaginative ways than simply allowing them to compound interest in the bank.

St. Andrew's in Ottawa, reaching into its financial reserves, established a $125,000 Good Neighbor Fund to "bring the church to the world and the world to the church." This good-works campaign supports visionary projects on the local scene, nationally, and overseas. They have worked with the Cooperative Development Foundation to establish a community-run banking and savings center, and to help train indigenous residents of the Northwest Territories to operate it. In Colombia, South America, they have supported a cooperative which enables women to assume financial responsibilities for families which have almost no income. And on the local scene they have helped Operation Go Home to expand their program aimed at getting kids off the streets.

People today want to do more than simply give their money to missions. They want to become involved themselves. A good example of this is St. Andrew's-Chalmers congregation in Uxbridge, Ontario. In 1987, the congregation purchased a house and planned to use it for seniors housing, a Christian day-care, or a book store. When these ideas fell through, they sold the house for a profit of $84,000. Interest from this money helped finance supplies for a group from the congregation who went to Guyana to assist the church there. This inspired the establishment of a fund, the interest from which is to be used to finance the purchase of supplies and equipment for two hands-on projects each year, one in Canada and one outside. After helping to rebuild a kitchen in l'Eglise St. Paul in Quebec, one member said about the St. Andrew's-Chambers group, "They even gave additional money to finish up odds and ends they were unable to complete. It was too much. We couldn't believe our good fortune."

As the number of refugees dramatically increases in the world, Presbyterian congregations are active in defending the rights of refugees and in helping many find new homes in Canada. Bridlewood Church in Agincourt, Ontario, launched a ministry to refugees in 1979. By 1990 the congregation had helped over 600 refugees settle in Canada. One of the original sponsors, Shirley Quinn, explains that, for her, this ministry grew naturally out of her church experience and gave her the opportunity to witness to the church's unique calling in the community. In her words, this means "not simply to help our own kind, but as the story of the Good Samaritan suggests, to go to those who are not like us."

Presbyterians from their beginning have stressed that the laity should play a significant role in the life of the church. Ruling elders lie at the heart of the Presbyterian system. Presbyterians should not need to be persuaded of the importance of getting everyone involved. But even Presbyterian congregations will sometimes slide into the rut of letting the clergy do it all and fail to call upon the creative gifts in their church families.

For many years, Cecilia and Ivan Dambrowitz have created their own summer programs for children. I had the privilege of seeing one in action during the summer of 1993 in the small village of Bluevale, Ontario. A large banner over the church announced a " summer adventure time." A member of the congregation who is a pilot and who has worked with televisions, turned the basement of the church into a spaceship. Every day, 70 children from the community climbed into this spaceship, with its flashing lights and humming motors, for a wonderful adventure. After viewing the spaceship following worship, an 80-year-old announced wistfully,

"I wish I could come." The whole community became involved and people who had not been touched by the church in years were suddenly moved through the enthusiasm of their children.

The message remains the same but we need to take the old stories and symbols and present them with a new immediacy. Oakridge Presbyterian Church in London, Ontario, accomplished this. Rather than celebrating Christmas with the usual Christmas pageant, they arranged for the congregation to revisit Bethlehem. A few weeks before Christmas, after a trumpet blast during Sunday morning worship, two soldiers dressed in full battle regalia, strode down the aisle and proclaimed that the congregation had been ordered to go to Bethlehem in the basement of the church on Friday night December 11. "Citizens who fail to sign in with their families," the stern soldiers warned, "will be prosecuted."

On the designated night, the congregation experienced, through taste, sight, and sound, Bethlehem as it might have been the night of Jesus' arrival. Terry Ingram, minister of Oakridge, summed things up at the end of the evening: "We have experienced things Jesus grew up seeing so long ago. Some things never change. The message of Christmas is always the same: God loves us."

First Presbyterian Church in Chatham, Ontario, took an event which occurs sometime in the life of every congregation and combined it with Reformed theology which declares that everyone's vocation can be a calling of God. During the summer of 1992, the congregation replaced the roof of their church. When the work was completed, they planned a service of appreciation for all those who had worked on the project. This included the contractors, the bank personnel, as well as those people who actually did the work. Some drove all the way from Toronto with their families for the service. Most said nothing like this had ever happened to them before.

This event witnessed to our faith which insists that, in our vocations, we also serve God. Or to paraphrase a comment made by Dorothy Sayers, the very first demand that religion makes upon the Christian carpenter is that he or she should make good tables.

Victoria-Royce church in Toronto creatively met their own need to have the brickwork of their building restored by providing work and training for the unemployed. Walter Moffat, an architect and member of the congregation, became the project coordinator. Mike

Plunkett, a master mason who had turned his life around by attending Alcoholics Anonymous meetings at Victoria-Royce, volunteered to train a number of unemployed area youth to do the work, at about 25 percent of the cost of a professional company. "We're carrying on a tradition at the church of putting people to work in hard times," Plunkett says.

In their quest for simplicity, Presbyterians have not always recognized nor affirmed the artistic gifts of their people. The arts, especially the visual arts, have sometimes been viewed with a mixture of suspicion and hostility. David Rankine is a talented artist who seeks to recover the old traditions by producing illuminations based on ancient Celtic Christian designs and motifs. Before most people were able to read, these intricate designs were used in a visual way to convey the biblical story. Rankine is convinced that images have a unique power to both inspire and instruct people in their faith. In 1994, the Presbyterian Church produced a wonderful, colorful poster featuring one of Rankine's pieces. Color and art is an area Presbyterians need to explore and use more fully.

Offering more than secondhand faith

Today the world demands more than secondhand faith from Christians. No longer will people, especially young people, be moved by what others have told them, or even by the authority of the Bible. They want to know, "How is it for you? What does it mean for you?"

A middle-aged woman brought the reality of this home to me. She called to ask if I would be willing to talk to someone who was not a member of my congregation. Jesting, I replied that, yes, sometimes I did—if really pressed. I should not have attempted to be humorous. The problem she faced was serious.

In conversation with her I discovered she had cancelled a scheduled gall bladder operation. The thought of the operation had turned her into a nervous wreck. She felt she could not go through with it. This, despite the fact that, from an outsider's point of view, she had met and overcome much greater obstacles than this.

In the midst of our conversation she suddenly fell silent. Then she raised her eyes and looked directly into mine. "Do you really believe in God," she asked. In the many years I had been a pastor, no one had ever put the question to me with such directness. I paused, and then replied softly, "Yes, on my good days." In the end she went through a successful operation. Today I look back on that incident as a harbinger of the future. Christians must learn and be prepared to share their own stories of faith.

The renewal movement called Cursillo has assisted many Presbyterians to do this. Cursillo is a Spanish word which means, literally, a short course. The initial weekend is viewed as a short course in Christianity.

In the late 1970s, Hamish Livingston worked for the Board of Congregational Life of the Presbyterian Church. He and Dalice, his wife, had attended a Roman Catholic Cursillo weekend which moved them. In 1979, he recruited a number of Presbyterians to experience a weekend, and the following year, with the help of some Roman Catholic friends, Cursillo was launched in the Presbyterian Church. This lay movement has since spread from the Maritimes to British Columbia. As Wilma Welsh, a longtime supporter of Cursillo puts it, "For many people it is the first time they understand experientially that God loves them."

As the state has taken over more and more of the social programs that the church provided in the past, some have wondered if any ministry would be left for congregations and individual Christians. In recent years, it has become clear that today's church faces more opportunities to provide caring ministries than ever before. With the breakdown of family life and relationships of all kinds, some people will not experience what it means to be a part of a family unless they experience it in the local congregation. The challenge of the vision document (pg. 159) for our denomination to become a family where all may find acceptance and love becomes particularly apt here.

A minister friend tells of visiting a woman in the hospital who was listed as a Presbyterian. "The Lord has sent you to me," she exclaimed. In fact, it turned out she was listed as a Presbyterian through a clerical error. After leaving the hospital, she joined a Bible study in my friend's church and soon became a member. When asked a short while later how things were going she replied, "Things at home are still difficult, but at least now I have friends."

Small cell groups can play a greater role as congregations

move from providing programs to supplying nurture and support for persons.

A large city church, St. John's in Cornwall, Ontario, has already experienced the power of small groups. Within these groups, people experience the care and support they need and long for, but which they never encounter in the larger congregation. Agnes Clark, a longtime member of St. John's, speaks of the joy of the faith many members have discovered in these groups.

More congregations are attempting to involve laypersons in the care of people in their congregations and communities, often through pastoral care committees or similar structures. In other words, they are attempting to recover the generosity, loving care, and forgiveness which have traditionally marked the life of the church.

Love with skin on it

The rural three-point charge of New Glasgow, Rodney, and Kintyre in southwestern Ontario has begun to train its members to care for each other and for their community. They describe what they're doing as "love with skin on it." Members of their pastoral ministry, known as the Outreach Ministry, pray for people under their care, contact them once a month by phone or letter, visit them at least four times a year, and assist in strengthening the relationships between the people in the district they serve. They also commit themselves to regular training sessions and a monthly reporting which ensures responsibility.

A contact person tells of a tender moment of love when the youngest member of a family in his care circle calls him "my church grandpa." Even in a rural setting, this kind of conscious effort in community building becomes necessary today.

I wish I could assure you that you could find all of the things I have talked about in every Presbyterian church. Of course that would be unrealistic.

In an article in the September newsletter of St. Andrew's Presbyterian Church in Kitchener, Ontario, the minister, Grant MacDonald, lists the things you can expect to find in his congregation. You should be able to find these things in **all** Presbyterian churches.

He begins by saying that here "the core beliefs of the Christian faith receive front-page attention." Among them he lists Christ crucified, dead and risen, the Bible as the revealed Word of God, the conviction that in the church people can discover and apply God's truth to their lives, and the hope of fulfillment of life after death in the communion of saints.

He goes on to say that you can expect to find a sense of community which is sensitive to the needs of the whole family. You can expect leaders who are aware of the issues of life and who will challenge your minds and wills with the gospel. Because congregations will increasingly be called upon to provide a caring ministry like they have never experienced before, you can expect to find hope and encouragement, but also to be turned outward to meet the needs in your community and world.

The Presbyterian contribution

The influence of Presbyterians in Canada has been both rich and varied. At a symposium held in Montreal in 1989 on the theme "The Presbyterian Contribution to Canadian Life and Culture," the claim was made that at least one-seventh of Canadian life is connected to the history of the Presbyterian Church.

That contribution has not always been viewed positively, especially by the popular press.

Writing in the *Presbyterian Record*, Lloyd Robertson, anchor for CTV news, recounts his shock upon hearing a remark on radio as he made his way to work one day. CBC radio's *As It Happens* was canvassing opinion on the debate over bilingualism. A woman listener said all problems relating to language and other concerns in the country were caused by the entrenched attitudes of those "White Anglo-Saxon Presbyterians." Not Protestants, but Presbyterians.

"As one connected...to the Presbyterian Church most of my life, I learned long ago we must share a terrible burden," Robertson wrote. The burden is the old argument "that the stolid, unbending, tight-fisted, puritanical ways of the Presbyterians are responsible for all the neuroses, most of the psychoses, and probably all of the warts endured by the average Canadian..."

Robertson concludes by asking, "So how are we to handle the old shibboleths that rain down on us on a regular basis? Just be happy that the very mention of the word 'Presbyterian' can evoke a range of responses from smirking to outrage to chilling disdain straight through to outright admiration. It means our forebears must have had an impact and done a lot of things well."

A large part of the Presbyterian contribution has been made and continues to be made in the academic and literary field. Robert Falconer, president of the University of Toronto from 1907 to 1932, and C. W. Gordon, better known by his writing name Ralph Connor, are two outstanding examples from history. Trevor Ferguson, Montreal novelist, and Margaret Avison, Toronto poet, are two contemporary examples.

Presbyterianism, first brought to this country over 400 years ago by French Huguenots and Scottish colonists, soon found itself in positions of influence and power at the center of life in the new land. Much has changed and the challenge for the Presbyterian Church today is whether it can adjust to its new position and role as a small and sometimes marginalized denomination in Canada. We frequently act as if we remain a large and influential denomination, trying to do everything and be represented on every ecumenical committee and task force. Sometimes we spread our limited resources so thinly we have little or no effect. We shall need to set priorities and impose limitations to allow us to make an effective witness to Jesus Christ from a Reformed perspective among our Christian brothers and sisters, as well as in the diverse and multicultural society in which we live.

Discovering life

I have spent almost all my life within the Presbyterian Church family. The Presbyterian Church is a denomination of conservative theology and liberal spirit. Within its life, I have been given the freedom to use my gifts, and to fall on my face. Its people have supported me in difficult times and celebrated with me in good times. In their midst I have discovered the truth of Mark Twain's words: "Heaven goes by favor. If it went by merit, you would stay out and your dog would go in." And finally, a host of loyal and loving friends in this church family have taught me the truth of Martin Luther's words: if God is our father, then surely the church is our mother. In her arms I have discovered life.

Study Guide
by Jim Taylor

Purpose

Let's be clear about the purpose for these sessions. It's to help people feel they belong to **this** community of people, **this** denomination, **this** church. It is **not** to transfer a dump truck full of information into their minds. So there are no correct answers to memorize, no tests to pass, no diplomas to hand out.

Many people recall their school years as a time of having to give the right answer; if they didn't have the right answer, it was wiser to keep their mouths shut. In church and in faith, right or wrong answers don't apply. Everyone—clergy, leaders, and lay participants—is on a journey of faith and growth together.

If, at the end of this time together, participants feel comfortable with each other and with what this church believes and does, the course will have been a success.

Learning principles

People today learn best by association. They test the new information they receive against what they already know from their own experience. If it fits, they keep it, and it becomes an integral part of the person. If it doesn't fit—or if there's no experience they can fit it to—they will soon forget it and lose it.

A key element of adult education, then, is to help participants identify experiences to which they can connect the new ideas.

Probably the best way to do this is through small group discussion. As people tell their own stories to each other, they bring their own experience out into the open. They have something to connect their learning to.

A lecture may allow a speaker to present a lot of information—but it doesn't give opportunity for the learners to assimilate that information, to integrate it with their most valuable resource, their own experience.

A group could be anything from two to eight persons. The larger the group, the more time it takes to involve everyone in discussing an idea. Above eight, the group is likely to split into two—either two separate discussions, or some who do all the talking and some who just listen. Those who "just listen" without contributing may never make the effort to find, in the library of their own experiences, the foundations on which to build their faith.

And because those foundations are experiences, there can be no right or wrong answers. One participant cannot say to another, "That wasn't what happened," or "Your experience was wrong." It's possible to offer an alternative experience, or a different interpretation of an experience, but not to challenge the experience itself. Life stories tend to evoke sympathy and compassion; judgment and disagreement usually result from generalized statements of principle or conviction.

Therefore we recommend

- using small groups
- involving everyone
- encouraging storytelling

Atmosphere

Because many adults (especially those over 40) may have painful memories of their school years, it's important to make the room itself feel friendly. Avoid, as far as possible, setups that look like a traditional classroom. Set chairs in a circle, or at least in a semi-circle—much as people would naturally sit in a living room, for example. Prefer comfortable chairs to uncomfortable ones.

Supply tea and coffee, juice, and cookies if you wish, and encourage people to help themselves. A bit of food and drink loosens things up. But don't let refreshments become a burden, where the suppliers feel they have to top the previous week's provisions.

Don't put anyone under pressure. If people don't want to join in small group discussion, don't force them. Participation must always be voluntary.

Ask participants to treat anything they hear in their groups as confidential.

Leadership

Leaders set the style for everyone else. Many people hesitate to share their own stories and experiences with others—they may fear laughter, or ridicule, or misunderstanding, or they may have been taught not to talk about themselves. A leader willing to risk being vulnerable, by including a few of his or her own experiences as sillustrations or examples, models the desired style for others.

At the same time, leaders should not be so personal as to draw all the attention to themselves. That models a style that encourages other participants also to try to dominate discussion, and may suggest that everyone else's faith journey is secondary.

Having a variety of people take leadership sets a good example for others.

Remember that participants often know less about their faith and their church than they like to admit. Churchy language may baffle them, or worse, alienate them. Explain church-related words and ideas—or better yet, use a story or personal anecdote to give these words meaning in context.

Since the purpose is to help people belong, not to get through a specified curriculum, leaders should not allow an agenda to dominate the sessions—other than to ensure that sessions start and end on time.

When participants really want to discuss a point, that's much more important than moving on to the next point just because the schedule says it's time.

Use questions, not authority, to direct or focus the discussion. Simple questions—sometimes even silly questions!—almost always stimulate discussion much better than complex ones. Avoid "closed" questions that ask for yes/no or right/wrong answers (unless you **want** to cut off discussion); use "open-ended" questions that ask for feelings or experiences.

Bibles

It's always a good idea for each member to have a Bible. (How much you use the Bible, in each session, will depend on the theological temperature of your congregation, but it's never a mistake to have Bibles available.) Encourage participants to use one of the modern translations: *The Good News Bible,* the *New Jerusalem Bible,* the *New International Version,* or the *New Revised Standard Version.* The old *King James Version* is a treasured part of our religious heritage, but the English language has changed so much since it was published, almost four centuries ago, that its wordings are as likely to conceal meaning as to reveal it. We recommend two relatively recent study Bibles, the *Harper-Collins Study Bible* or the *New Oxford Annotated Bible*, for those wanting to explore texts more deeply.

Typical format of a session

1. Informal **gathering time**: People are free to stand around, chat, etc.
2. **Opening**: 5–10 minutes to reduce tensions and get people comfortable with each other. Familiar songs can do this; so can simple exercises and activities related to the theme of the session. You may find additional useful suggestions in the "icebreakers" in *The Whole People of God's "Adult Study"* paks.
3. **Input**: By expressing the message of a chapter in his or her own words, a leader introduces participants to the theme for the evening and gets them thinking. About 15 minutes maximum. Remember that this is not a sermon opportunity.
4. **Brainstorming**: A short period, perhaps 5 minutes, which encourages people to bring forth ideas and reactions without fear of contradiction or challenge.
5. **Discussion**: in small groups, of suggested questions for about 30 minutes.
6. **Feedback**: Responses from small groups—not reports of what they discussed, but of what they learned from each other and, perhaps, what difference this will make in their lives. 10–15 minutes, depending on the size of group.
7. **Closing**: Inform participants of chapters they should read for the next session. Prayer or music. Keep it brief: 2–3 minutes.

The number and timing of sessions

This study guide suggests five sessions, each running approximately 90 minutes. There's nothing magic about the number five—you might choose to do fewer sessions, or you might choose to use the pattern here to create additional sessions, based on other chapters in the book.

The sessions could be held on a series of evenings. Or you could, without much adapting, run them over a weekend, from Friday evening to Sunday afternoon.

Session 1 (Chapters 1 and 2)
Who are we, anyway?

Opening: Welcome the participants. Explain anything necessary about confidentiality, getting coffee, cleaning up, etc.
Lead in an opening prayer, such as the following:
Dear God, you have chosen and called us to be your people. You have made us members of your church. Give us a sense of who we are, so that we can live more effectively as your witnesses to the world. Bless your church. Keep it focused clearly on the good news of Jesus Christ, and let it be a place where all are warmly welcomed and included in your community of joy, peace, and love. Amen.

Opening activity: Do **one or more** of the following.
a) sing some favorite songs related to the theme of belonging, such as #44, *Part of the family,* from *Songs for a Gospel People*, or #302, *The church is wherever*, from *The Book of Praise*.
b) make up name tags that show
— the person's name
— the person's origin (place or denomination, or both)
c) ask people, in groups of 2–4, to talk about their earliest memories of church or Sunday school. What makes those things memorable?

Input: A leader—not necessarily clergy—who has read the book and distilled the main points of chapters 1 and 2, talks about what makes **this** congregation in **this** denomination special for him or her. Highlight or underline not more than six quotations in the chapters that are likely to provoke discussion. You don't have to agree with them all—in fact, it's good if the leader doesn't agree with everything in the book, as that frees the participants also to find their own viewpoints—but do not choose quotations simply so that you can dispute them!

If you wish to include a biblical base, look first at the lectionary readings for this week, to see if any of them offer insights. Alternatively, consider 1 Peter 2:9–10 or Deuteronomy 7:6–8.

Brainstorming: Invite participants to call out what makes **this** congregation in **this** denomination special for them. Encourage people to volunteer ideas quickly.

Remember that in brainstorming, no one is ever right or wrong—if one person likes this congregation for its conservative theology, and another for its liberal theology, they're both right. Put both answers up!) The purpose of this brainstorming is not to reach any kind of consensus, or even to identify any common themes (though it's nice if they appear) but to set up an expectation that anyone can present any idea.

Have someone write the suggestions up quickly on a board or flipchart for future reference, if necessary.

Discussion: If there are eight or more people, divide into sub-groups. Ask each group to discuss questions such as these:

- *What kinds of people does this congregation particularly attract?*
- *What stories do you know about the origins of this congregation?*
- *Who do you think of as a dominant influence in shaping the faith/ theology of this congregation? What do you know about him/her?*
- *What does it mean to you to be "a chosen race, a royal priesthood... God's own people"?* (1 Peter 2:9)

Tip: Leaders of discussion groups are there to keep discussion moving and to prevent any individuals from dominating. As far as possible, discourage people from citing memorized Bible verses or doctrinal assertions, as these tend to cut off any further discussion. If such responses do occur, ask a supplementary question, such as, "Was there some particular time in your life when that message took on particular meaning for you?"

Feedback: Not a report on what was discussed, but what was learned from the discussion. Some people may want to share individual insights; others may want to identify some (often vague) emerging consensus.

Closing: Depending on time and the inclinations of the group, close with a suitable song and/or prayer. Invite people to consume the last of the refreshments. Don't hurry people out—some of the most valuable discussion may take place after the formal part of the session is over.

Session 2 (Chapters 8 and 9)
Our ways of worshiping

Because this session focuses on patterns and practices of worship, you might want to invite your minister(s) and a member of the worship committee (or its equivalent) to attend this session.

Opening: Distribute name tags again. If you didn't use denominational origin last time, add it to the name tag this time.

Do **one or more** of the following to get people talking about their experience of worship in church:

a) Do a chain interview. Set up two rows of chairs, enough for everyone present, facing each other. Hand out sheets that contain questions such as these:

- *When did you first have communion?*
- *How old were you when you were baptized?*
- *What used to make you fidget most?*
- *Was your minister male or female?*
- *Did you go to church Sunday morning, or Sunday evening, or ...?*
- *What else was there to do on Sunday?*
- *How did you get to church?*
- *How did they keep the church warm in winter?*
- *What hymns do you remember singing?*
- *How much did you put in the offering plate in those days?*

There should be at least as many questions as people. Have the people sit on the chairs, facing each other. They ask each other the first question, and note their answers. Then everyone moves one seat to the right, and asks the next question of the person now facing them, and so on, until you run out of time or all questions have been answered.

b) In groups of three or four—but **never** individually—have people create a collective mural of worship as they remember it from their childhood. It doesn't matter if they can't agree enough to produce a finished piece of art; the task is simply an excuse to get people visualizing their early worship context. Provide any supplies needed: newsprint, crayons, colored markers, magazines, glue...

c) Music, preferably familiar pieces whose words or tunes lend themselves to the theme of this session.

Input: One or more members of the leadership team (which can include participants) who have read the book and distilled the main points of chapters 8 and 9, talks about how **this** congregation in **this** denomination typically worships.

Highlight or underline up to six quotations in the chapters that are likely to provoke discussion. It's helpful to choose references that may have been new insights for you, or that reinforced previous understandings. Remember that this is not a learned lecture—it's a way of sharing what makes worship special and meaningful for you.

If you wish to include a biblical base, look first at the lectionary readings for this week, to see if any of them offer insights. Alternatively, consider Psalms 96, 98, or 100, or Exodus 20:8–11; from the New Testament, Matthew 12:1–8 for why Christians worship on Sunday rather than Saturday, the Jewish sabbath, or 1 Corinthians 11:23–26, the central ritual of Christian worship.

Brainstorming: Invite the participants to call out all the questions they ever had about worship, but never had the courage to ask. Write them up on a board or flipchart for further reference. At this time, don't attempt to answer the questions—simply identify them. Treat all questions seriously, no matter how trivial some may seem.

Discussion: in small groups.

Invite the groups to select three or four questions from the list for discussion. See what responses they can generate from

- their own wisdom and experience
- the book
- the expertise of the minister(s) and worship committee members.

If necessary, supplement the questions listed by the group with other questions such as these:

- *If you had to shorten a service, what part(s) would you cut? Why?*
- *What kind of role do laypeople play in our congregation's worship?*
- *How often do we celebrate communion (or the Eucharist, the Mass, or the Lord's Supper)? Why do we follow that practice?*
- *What is the oldest (or most historic) component in our worship services?*
- *What do you think God might consider "a joyful noise unto the Lord"?*

Feedback: Ask what people have learned about their worship services during this session? What do they now value more than they used to?

Closing: Assign the chapters for the next session. Close with prayer, or music, or both.

Session 3 (Chapters 4 and 10)
The rest of the week

Opening: Distribute name tags. Introduce any newcomers to the old-timers, and vice versa.

Do **one or more** of the following, depending on time and interest:
a) Distribute sheets of paper. Issue a challenge—to see who can create the longest list of community or local organizations that the members of this group are active in, **excluding your own activities and associations**. When time is up, share the lists, wonder about the number of organizations and causes this congregation supports in one way or another, and give a round of applause to the person who gathered the longest list. (Note: it's okay to include church activities and organizations. It can be interesting, however, to circle the church-related activities, to see to what extent interests are focused exclusively inward or outward.)
b) Form a "common link" chain. Each person joins hands with someone in a similar organization. So a hockey coach who has subscription tickets

to the symphony takes the hand of a hockey parent on one side and a high school music teacher on the other. Remember that each person has two hands, and probably a dozen possible links. The idea is to get everyone connected to someone else. Expect bedlam as people make and break the chain to accommodate others and get a maximum of people involved.
c) Appropriate music.

Input: Someone who has read chapters 4 and 10 and digested the main points should expand, for 10 minutes or so, on what it means to be a Christian for the rest of the week, Monday through Saturday. How does that person live his or her faith in the daily dilemmas of work and family and leisure? Again, a few good, provocative quotations from the book will help, but don't let the talk become simply a summary of the book.

To incorporate biblical teaching, first check the lectionary readings for the week. If those don't relate well, try Micah 6:8, Matthew 26:31–45, or 1 Corinthians 12:4–27.

Brainstorm: In a church group, some people may be hesitant to say what they personally think of the church. But they'll almost always be able to say what they think others are saying about the church!

Ask: "What do people say about the church—the Christian church in general, and this church in particular?" Write the comments on a board or flipchart.

Tip: When fielding "brainstormed" ideas, watch out for persistent trends. That is, if all the comments are positive, you might need to say, "Aren't there people who claim the church is full of hypocrites?" or "What about the claim that the church is always asking for money?" Similarly, if the trend seems to emphasize negative aspects of the church, plant ideas that may generate some positive responses: "What do they say about our Food Bank?" or "I've heard that people love our choir."

Discussion: Using the book, chapters 4 and 10, identify and list the social issues on which your church has taken a stand. Do not discuss them yet—just list them.

Have each small group (if you have divided into small groups) choose one issue they would like to discuss in more depth. As well as considering the biblical or theological rationale for that stand, compare how that stand relates to people's attitudes about the church, identified in the brainstorming period. (For example, if the issue chosen is "remarriage of divorced persons," compare that to a perception of the church as, say, "a closed and exclusive club.")

Feedback: Ask people to identify what they found comforting about this session's discussion, and what they found disturbing.

Closing: Assign chapters to read for the next session. Close with music or prayer or both.

Session 4 (Chapters 3 and 7)
What we believe

Please note: this session does not attempt to define what any person or congregation should believe. It intends merely to help participants identify what they believe, and to see how those beliefs fit together in a congregational pattern.

Opening: Name tags. Introductions of any newcomers.

Put out some jigsaw puzzles on tables before the session. Invite early arrivers to play with the puzzles. Children's puzzles—perhaps borrowed from the Sunday school—can be done relatively quickly and cleared away. Avoid complicated puzzles that will distract people's attention from the session itself.

Do **one or more** of the following:

a) Appropriate music to build community.

b) Have people place themselves on a continuum, according to their theological views. Draw an imaginary line along the floor. Define one end as theologically conservative, the other end as theologically liberal/radical. If there's any fuss over definitions, just ask people to place themselves along the line according to **their** definition of liberal or conservative, in relation to others whom they know. Expect a fair amount of jiggling and switching of places, as people find themselves more radical than Jim or more conservative than Luella.

This may be the first time some people have identified themselves by their theology. Invite some feedback, as the group sits for the Input section.

c) Hand out a sheet with a number of metaphors for God listed on it, such as the following. Make sure there's a good mix of metaphors. Ask people to rank those metaphors according to their own preferences, and then to compare their rankings with at least one other person.

A mother hen with her chicks
A king with a golden crown sitting on a throne
A mighty wind
A fire raging out of control
A still small voice
A mighty and victorious conqueror
A farmer sowing seeds
An eagle soaring above the earth
A fishing net
A thief in the night
A city
A river
A tree
A woman cleaning her house
A member of an unpopular ethnic minority
A judge sentencing a criminal
A spouse discovering a partner's adultery
A candle burning in the night
A gardener pruning vines

A trickle of blood
A mother mourning a lost child
A potter working clay
A person doing laundry

Input: This talk probably comes as close to a traditional lecture as any. Someone needs to go over chapters 3 and 7, identifying "turning points" in the shaping of the faith to which this congregation belongs. Who were some of the key figures? Why were they significant? What difference do they still make to us today? However, the speaker doing the summarizing should try to avoid sounding like an authority; he or she should admit, "Until I read this book, I hadn't realized that..." or "I realize I hadn't thought much about..."

For a biblical emphasis, check first the lectionary readings for the week; or consider 1 Corinthians 1:22–25, Isaiah 55:6–9, Deuteronomy 6:4–5 (with Matthew 22:37, Mark 12:29–30, or Luke 10:27).

Brainstorm: Ask people to develop a "job description" for an absolutely ideal member of this church. What would that person have to do? What would that person have to believe? Don't worry if some of the responses are contradictory—write them on the board or flipchart anyway.

Try to keep people out of self-imposed ruts. If all the comments deal with church activities, ask, "What about his/her family life?" If the comments lean to the financial side, ask, "Doesn't anyone need a Sunday school teacher?" If the requirements all tend to be practical, ask, "So this person doesn't have to believe in God?"

Discussion: in your group(s), do one or both of the following:
a) Try to narrow the list of "job requirements" down to no more than a half-dozen points. Discuss how those are biblically or traditionally sound—or why the Bible and tradition don't apply in this instance.
b) Discuss questions such as these:

- *What does it feel like to fall head-over-heels in love? Have you ever felt that way about God?*
- *What kind of world did your grandparents grow up in? How different is it from your world today?*
- *If being Christian were a crime, would there be enough evidence to convict you?*
- *If the Christian faith was a treasure that could be contained in a big box, what kind of role would you play in relation to that treasure box?* (Examples: guard, box polisher, scout warning of danger, prospector seeking new treasures to add, ticket seller for gawking tourists, someone handing it out to those in need, professor studying it, etc.)

Feedback: What have people learned about their faith and church today? What difference will it make in their lives? (Remember that it's not the **facts** people have learned that matters, but their **relationship** to those historical facts and doctrines.)

Closing: Music and prayer are always suitable. We suggest, for this session, saying together one of the historic statements of Christian faith such as the Nicene or Apostles' Creeds or any credal statement approved by the church.

Session 5 (Chapter 11)
Commitment to ministry

This session anticipates closing with a communion or symbolic agape meal. For that, you will need to prepare in advance bread and wine/juice.

Opening: Name tags and introductions, as appropriate.

Do **one or more** of the following:

a) Sing again some of the songs you have used in other sessions.

b) Make up a group of name tags, of fairly well-known people in the church, locally, nationally, internationally, or historically. Stick a name onto each person's back. People have to find out the name on their back by asking questions about that person's ministry. Most questions should be answerable with yes or no. (Possible examples: Mother Teresa ministers to the sick and dying in Calcutta; Jim Taylor's ministry is writing; Michael Peers is the senior archbishop in the Anglican Church of Canada; Susie Dobbs works as a volunteer in the Food Bank.)

c) Try a variant on the children's game of "whisper a message around the circle." Choose a simple sentence of six or so words—not a favorite verse from the Bible. Say it to the first person in the circle, so that everyone can hear it. That person changes just one word in that sentence and passes it on to the next person. No one may repeat a change that someone else made already.

An example might go like this:

I love pickles on my hamburgers.
*I **hate** pickles on my hamburgers.*
*I hate pickles on **your** hamburgers.*
*I hate pickles on your **raincoat**.*
***You** hate pickles on your raincoat.*

The point, if anyone doesn't get it, is how each person's contribution, though it may seem small, affects the message.

Input: With reference to chapter 11, try to identify the particular ministry that you feel God is calling **this** congregation, in **this** place, in **this** denomination, to perform. Admit that this is your view, and that others may not agree. Include some stumbling blocks and potholes that may prevent this congregation from accomplishing its ministry.

Remember that you're not talking about someone "out there," but about the ministry of these people, right here, right now, who have studied and struggled with you for the last five sessions.

For biblical connections, check the lectionary passages for this week, or see Mark 1:16–20, Romans 12:3–8, Jeremiah 31:31–34, Luke 4:17–20, or Luke 8:1–3.

Brainstorm: What other ideas can people come up with, to identify the ministry of this congregation, in this place, with these resources, at this time? Include the ideas presented during the Input part of the program. (Remember to list all ideas, no matter how unlikely, and do not allow anyone to argue with any of the ideas offered. If someone doesn't like a suggestion, invite them to offer an alternate.)

Discussion: In your group(s), discuss questions such as these:

- *What's a ministry?*
- *Who has a ministry?*
- *Who ministers to me? How?*

Feedback: Instead of asking for feedback in the usual way, ask everyone to take five minutes in silence, to look at the ideas on the board or flipchart, to choose just one item from that list where they can make a difference, and to commit themselves to start making that difference. Have each person write that commitment on a slip of paper, for use in the closing act of worship.

Closing: If you have a communion service or agape meal, bring in the elements. Remind people that historically, these elements were gifts from the people's own fields and orchards. Suggest that along with these symbolic gifts, we need to add our real and present commitments.

As part of the service, formal or informal, invite each person in turn to place the slip of paper with his or her commitment on it on the table beside the bread and wine/juice. Those who are willing could read out their commitment, thus going public with it.

Close with a communion prayer, or a prayer such as this:

Gracious God, we thank you for the time we have shared together in this study of our faith. Continue to work in us, to make us the people you have chosen us to be. Give us opportunities for ministry, as you see fit. Equip us to serve you faithfully and well, and give us joy in our service. Enable us to trust you, always, in what you have done for us and all people through Jesus. Amen.

Credits: prayers and some Bible readings by Kenn Ward; other readings and activities suggested by Bev Milton, Norma Goughnour, and Marilyn Perry.

A Vision

1. We will grow in our relationship with Jesus Christ.
2. We will reach out in mission, proclaiming the Good News of Jesus Christ with relevance and power.
3. We will integrate evangelism, social action, and justice ministry.
4. Our congregations will be alive.
5. We will be a loving, inclusive community—truly God's family.
6. We will be effective communicators.
7. We will have a Spirit-led ministry by the whole people of God.
8. The courts of the Church will be vital and compassionate.
9. The administration of the Church will be lean and accountable.

—The Presbyterian Church in Canada
adopted by the 115th General Assembly

Resources for further study and reflection

Book of Forms. Contains all of the regulations which govern all of the courts of The Presbyterian Church in Canada.

The Book of Common Worship. The Presbyterian Church in Canada, 1991. Contains orders of services and prayers for the church year and special occasions.

Clifford, Keith. *The Resistance to Church Union in Canada*. University of British Columbia Press, 1985. Clifford, a former professor of religious studies at the University of British Columbia and United churchman, offers a sympathetic perspective of those Presbyterians who resisted Church Union in 1925.

The Discipleship Team of the Life and Mission Agency of the Presbyterian Church have produced a series of attractive and useful pamphlets including: "The Presbyterian Church in Canada: A Thinking Church with a Tender Heart," "Faith Commitment: A Matter of Choice," "Membership Commitment," and a series of seven: "Presbyterians are People Who Worship... Who Share... Who Follow Jesus Christ... Who Pray,,, Who Care About Justice... Who Serve... Who Grow in Faith."

Farris, Stephen. "Reformed Identity and Reformed Worship," an article in *Reformed World*, March & June, 1993. This helpful article outlines some of the main characteristics of Presbyterian worship.

Frontiers. A 17-minute video with guide. Provides a brief history of The Presbyterian Church in Canada.

Hayes, Stephen. *The Presbyterian Church Upside Down.* Resource Distribution, 1979. A 40-page booklet on the worship and beliefs of the Presbyterian Church.

Heritage Resources. This vast array of resources on the history, life, and faith of the Presbyterian Church comes in several kits and was originally published by the Board of Congregational Life. Unfortunately this resource is now out of print, so you will have to borrow it from someone.

Klempa, William, editor. *The Burning Bush and a Few Acres of Snow.* Carlton University Press, 1994. Essays on the Presbyterian contribution to Canadian life and culture from symposiums held at Presbyterian College, Montreal, in October 1988, and Knox College, Toronto, May 1989.

Living Faith: A statement of Christian Belief. Wood Lake, 1984. A modern statement of faith adopted by the Presbyterian Church as an acceptable statement and useful for both worship and study. This statement has found wide acceptance throughout the church.

Moir, John. *Enduring Witness: A History of The Presbyterian Church in Canada.* Committee on Church History, Revised edition, 1987. The most comprehensive and readable history of The Presbyterian Church in Canada commissioned originally for the 100th anniversary of the church in 1975.

Moir, John and W. Stanford Reid, editors. *Called to Witness: Profiles of Canadian Presbyterians.* Published by the Committee on History, 1975, 1980, and 1991. These three softcover books written by a variety of authors offer interesting profiles of Canadian Presbyterians.

Social Action Handbook. Includes all the social action statements and recommendations of General Assembly arranged topically in loose-leaf format. Updates provided annually.

Woensdregt, Yme. *Public Worship: Something We Do.* The Presbyterian Church in Canada, 1994.